PRAISE FOR BRIGHT COMPLEX KIDS

"Peterson and Peters have written a practical guide exploring the topics that are most important in learning about, and understanding, bright children. I always know a resource book is valuable when reading it makes me think about students I know and how it would help them make better sense of themselves. Educators, parents, and mental health professionals will learn more about what bright students need from us and can use ideas from this book to support and nurture increased self-awareness in gifted youth. The authors help us to discern pitfalls of misdiagnosing what it truly is that these young people need us to know about them, so that they may 'be seen' and thrive."

—Terry Bradley, M.A., gifted education consultant and past president,
Colorado Association for Gifted and Talented

"In *Bright, Complex Kids*, gifted education experts Drs. Jean Sunde Peterson and Daniel B. Peters combine their vast experience and wisdom as practitioners and scholars to coauthor a fantastic resource for parents and others invested in understanding the unique social and emotional needs and concerns of high-ability youth. Engaging, informative, and practical, this book will surely be a favorite on the readers' bookshelf. Filled with keen insights, useful suggestions and strategies, and relevant case examples that bring the content to life, *Bright, Complex Kids* is a treasure trove of information and truly a delight to read. I don't like this book—I LOVE it!"

— Michelle C. Muratori, Ph.D., senior counselor at Johns Hopkins
Center for Talented Youth and faculty associate at Johns Hopkins School of Education

"Great things happen when a well-respected scholar joins a clinical psychologist in collaborating on a project that involves a shared passion. Peterson and Peters have done just that. Through their insights, shared experiences, and scholarship, the authors bring a deep understanding of how to support the social and emotional development of highly able children and teens. Grounded in contemporary theory and research, filled with practical suggestions for teachers, counselors, and families, and delivered in an accessible writing style, *Bright, Complex Kids* will serve as an informative resource for all who work with children and teens with high ability."

—Thomas P. Hébert, Ph.D., professor, Gifted and Talented Education, University of South Carolina

"*Bright, Complex Kids* is the book I have been waiting for! Written by two esteemed names in gifted education, this book shares with us combined treasures of wisdom from two colleagues who have grown a lasting friendship around both their shared and divergent experiences with bright and gifted children, adolescents, and adults. While predominantly a book for parents, any counselor, teacher or other caregiver will find this beautifully written and highly readable book full of helpful information, touching case studies, seasoned insight, and encouraging guidance for understanding and nurturing the bright and gifted they care about and love. Each chapter is a gem, and the combined work is an exceptionally rich and welcoming read. I cannot wait to tell my colleagues, friends, students and clients about this book!"

—Debra Mishak, Ph.D., PSC, Winona State University, and private practitioner counseling gifted and talented teens and adults

"*Bright, Complex Kids* is a gift to the field of gifted education. Within the pages of their book, Dr. Peterson and Dr. Peters offer educators, clinical professionals, and caregivers a masterful course in understanding and nurturing the affective needs of high-ability children. Their book is filled with gentle reminders and research-based strategies (many informed by their own research) that will help adults truly open themselves to learning about the complex nature of high ability. Through a nonjudgmental and strengths-focused approach, the authors guide adults in how to meaningfully engage and interact with high-ability children. They offer hands-on strategies that are intended not only to empower bright, complicated kids, but also the caring adults in their lives."

—Jennifer A. Ritchotte, Ph.D., associate professor, co-coordinator of Gifted & Talented Graduate Programs, and director of the Center for Gifted and Talented Education, University of Northern Colorado, and coauthor of *Start Seeing and Serving Underserved Gifted Students*

"Jean Peterson and Dan Peters have created an important book with practical advice for parents and teachers about authentically relating to gifted children and youth and helping them with their emotional issues. *Bright, Complex Kids* is a unique blend of the authors' counseling and clinical insights, embedded in Jean Peterson's stellar empirical research. The authors urge readers to learn from the children themselves and 'embrace their awesome complexity.' Highlights of the book are Jean's asset-burden paradox and Dan's Worry Monster. This excellent resource should be in every doctor's office and is recommended for parent book clubs."

—Linda Kreger Silverman, Ph.D., licensed psychologist, founder, Gifted Development Center/ISAD

"Jean Peterson and Dan Peters have spent decades working with—and *learning from*—bright and complex kids. This book synthesizes their knowledge and compassionate understanding to provide insights into the hearts, minds, and experiences of these bright, talented, and creative youth. The two authors share stories from the lives of the children they have worked with, and they provide resources, recommendations, and guidance for those who know, care about, love—and sometimes are confounded by—them. I can't recommend this book highly enough!"

—Dr. Susan Daniels, cofounder and educational director of Summit Center, associate dean of Bridges Graduate School, and author of *Visual Learning and Teaching*

BRIGHT, COMPLEX KIDS

Supporting Their Social and Emotional Development

Jean Sunde Peterson, Ph.D.
Daniel B. Peters, Ph.D.

free spirit
PUBLISHING®

Library of Congress Cataloging-in-Publication Data
Names: Peterson, Jean Sunde, 1941– author. | Peters, Daniel B., 1970– author.
Title: Bright, complex kids : supporting their social and emotional development / Jean Sunde Peterson and Daniel B. Peters.
Description: Minneapolis, MN : Free Spirit Publishing Inc., 2021. | Includes bibliographical references and index.
Identifiers: LCCN 2020049198 (print) | LCCN 2020049199 (ebook) | ISBN 9781631985867 (paperback) |
    ISBN 9781631985874 (pdf) | ISBN 9781631985881 (epub)
Subjects: LCSH: Gifted children—Education. | Gifted children—Counseling of. | Affective education.
Classification: LCC LC3993.2 .P479 2021 (print) | LCC LC3993.2 (ebook) | DDC 371.95—dc23
LC record available at https://lccn.loc.gov/2020049198
LC ebook record available at https://lccn.loc.gov/2020049199

ISBN: 978-1-63198-586-7

Edited by Christine Zuchora-Walske
Cover and interior design by Shannon Pourciau

10 9 8 7 6 5 4 3 2 1
Printed in the United States of America

Free Spirit Publishing Inc.
6325 Sandburg Road, Suite 100
Minneapolis, MN 55427-3674
(612) 338-2068
help4kids@freespirit.com
freespirit.com

FSC
www.fsc.org
MIX
Paper from
responsible sources
FSC® C005010

DEDICATION

To my parents, for modeling countless positives; to Reuben, for supporting me and my work unconditionally over all of our decades; and to Sonia and Nathan, who don't fit the stereotypes.

—Jean

To my parents, for their unyielding support; to Liz, who is my partner in everything; and to Sadie, Joe, and Tobie, who have taught me so much.

—Dan

ACKNOWLEDGMENTS

We especially want to thank our editor, Christine Zuchora-Walske, for her careful attention to content, quick responses during our rhythmical three-way e-communication during the various editing stages, and her broad editorial expertise. We appreciate her understanding of bright kids—and her willingness to challenge us. She prodded us to step back and make sure nuances were clear and accurate. We are also grateful for the expertise at Free Spirit of Meg Bratsch, project developer; Alyssa Lochner, production editor; Shannon Pourciau, designer; and the content-review team in the final stages of editing.

We also want to acknowledge Bobbie Gilman for expertly reviewing our 2e chapter. We are grateful for Linda Silverman's careful and thoughtful review of the misdiagnosis chapter and for her skilled guidance regarding the complexities of 2e children.

In addition, we acknowledge each other's role in moving us toward this book project. We remember clearly when we first became acquainted at conferences and conventions, realizing that our differing professional paths and preparation did not preclude our being kindred spirits focused on listening to, and honoring, the inner world of bright kids—the "whole child." When we eventually copresented sessions or were panelists together, we smiled over the synergy we felt. That positive generativity has continued, and as a result, creating this book was inspiring and satisfying.

Contents

Introduction

CHILDREN and teens with high ability are "different"—different enough from age peers that programs are developed to address their needs and concerns. Their exceptionality affects all aspects of life—not just intellectually, but also socially and emotionally. When they or their parents seek help, however, the professionals they consult may have had little or no formal preparation for working with this complicated, highly idiosyncratic population. For example, school counselors very rarely get pertinent information about high-ability kids (Peterson and Wachter Morris 2010). Even the brightest professionals may be unaware of perspectives that could help them relate comfortably and effectively with highly capable children and teens. This practical, user-friendly book begins to fill that information gap.

A bell curve is often used to illustrate how intellectual ability is distributed in the general population. See the diagram "Distribution of Intellectual Ability" on page 2 (Davidson Institute for Talent Development 2020). The highest section of the curve represents the largest percentage of the population—the middle or average range of ability. The curve on either side tapers to the smallest percentages—the lowest and highest levels of ability. At each end of the curve are people who differ greatly from those with average ability. Noteworthy is that individuals at one end, with exceptionally high ability, are as far from the middle, and are as different from the middle, as those at the other end. Children and teens at both ends warrant, and can benefit from, special services in education.

> Individuals with exceptionally high ability are as far from the middle, and are as different from the middle, as are those at the other end. Children and teens at both ends warrant, and can benefit from, special services in education.

This book is about the high-ability children and teens who are in the upper end of the curve. We include some information about kids with exceptionally high ability, but our main focus is on high ability in broad terms—beyond just the top 2 to 3 percent. We will often refer to "bright" or "high-ability kids" in the same generic way that the gifted-education field refers to "gifted kids," because we want to help our readers understand options, policies, and constraints, regardless of how they were established, whether they make sense, and whether they seem fair. We will indeed be referring to children and teens whose abilities fit into the upper area of the bell curve. However, our descriptions, explanations, and examples will also reflect what we have seen in bright kids who cannot (because of disabilities or other personal circumstances) or will not (because of developmental hurdles or a cultural valuing of wisdom, not knowledge) demonstrate their ability through classroom or test performance.

High ability can be both an asset and a burden, both a strength and a vulnerability. This book is about that paradox—and the importance of understanding and supporting bright children and teens.

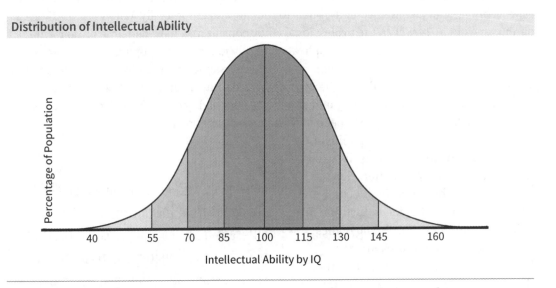

Distribution of Intellectual Ability

Percentage of Population (y-axis)

40   55   70   85   100   115   130   145   160

Intellectual Ability by IQ

WHY WE WROTE THIS BOOK

We believe that parents and guardians, grandparents, classroom teachers, school adminis-trators, directors, coaches, school and community counselors, school and other psycholo-gists, professors, undergraduate and graduate students, youth program leaders, and others who interact with children and teens need a user-friendly book to help them make sense of school-age kids with high ability—and, perhaps, of themselves as well. We wrote this book to share what we have learned about the concerns, needs, and social and emotional devel-opment of this complex, widely varying demographic group. We drew from our teaching and clinical work to show how various concepts and characteristics are applied or demon-strated. We make suggestions about what invested adults can do to support bright indi-viduals, regardless of their performance on standardized tests and in the classroom, and regardless of socioeconomic and other personal circumstances, including disabilities. To gain enough trust for a comfortable, constructive relationship with highly able children and their families, adults need particular skills, knowledge, and awareness.

We have worked with high-ability kids and their families for many years. Dan is a psychologist, consultant, advocate, and author focused largely on bright children and adolescents. Jean, though officially retired as a counselor and researcher, continues to work as a consultant, speaker, author, and creator of social and emotional curricula. For many years, we paid attention to each other's work, realized how in sync our perspectives are, copresented at conferences a few times, and appreciated each other's passionate investment in the social and emotional development of highly able kids. After discussing this book project for several years, we finally decided to commit fully to it.

The perspectives we offer are based on our experiences in our various professional roles and as parents. Jean's observations during twenty years of classroom teaching, and fifteen concurrent years with a summer foreign-language day camp she and her husband directed, informed her subsequent years of teaching high-ability adolescents. In the high school gifted-education program she eventually directed, development-related small-group discussions with students inspired her to pursue master's and doctoral degrees in counseling and counselor education at the University of Iowa, where she was supported by a fellowship in the Belin-Blank Center for Gifted Education and Talent Development. Her clinical work and consulting there led to her second career, as a counselor and an educator of counselors. Her cross-disciplinary research continues to inform the gifted-education and counselor-education fields about each other.

Dan's doctorate in clinical psychology is applied at the multisite Summit Center in California, which he cofounded and directs, focused on bright children and adolescents. He shares his perspectives, based on his extensive clinical practice, through the informative Summit Center website; through his own consulting and conference presentations and workshops; through his books, blogs, and podcasts; and through Camp Summit.

In addition to our hands-on work with high-ability children and teens, we have stayed current through formal professional development, reviewing journal manuscripts, and receiving feedback after our consultations and presentations. Giants in the fields of counseling and clinical psychology, many of whom are cited and discussed in this book, grabbed our attention early, and we are indebted to them. Those who paid attention to our work along the way, such as James Webb, Michael Piechowski, and Linda Silverman, nudged us forward. In this book we share what we have learned.

We hope our book helps readers not only feel more informed, but also feel more competent and confident. Our focus is on what we believe adults need to know about bright children and teens, as well as on what caring adults might do to engage them meaningfully. We are painfully aware that many bright kids do not feel understood or supported. Many who have high ability are not perceived as smart because they do not demonstrate behaviors that teachers believe reflect giftedness, such as verbal assertiveness, contributing to discussions, compliance, strong social skills, or high academic performance. A learning disability, anxiety, depression, learning English as a new language, difficult family circumstances, and cultural values, for example, may inhibit those behaviors. As a result, some high-ability students are not identified as eligible for special programs.

Regardless of how bright they are, how well they achieve academically, or whether they are identified for special programming, highly able children and teens are like their age peers in some ways. They all face developmental challenges as they grow and change, and they may face dangerous, toxic, unstable, insecure life situations. However, the sensitivity inherent in high ability may exacerbate how bright kids experience and respond to developmental challenges, life circumstances, and environmental stimuli. In this book, we offer ideas about how invested adults can interact comfortably and effectively with them while gaining entrance to their internal world, including how to listen and respond, how to self-monitor adult biases, how to avoid communicating awe of high ability because of the potential impact on trust and openness, how to apply knowledge of learning disabilities, and how to help high-ability children and teens make sense of themselves.

Various books are available that address some of the topics we address. However, many of these books for teachers, clinicians, and researchers are too large, unwieldy, academic, and expensive for easy purchase, reference, and application. We offer our book as a useful, efficient, and practical bridge to the social, emotional, and cognitive world of highly capable kids.

ABOUT THIS BOOK

The chapter titles in this book are all active, because bright kids and the adults in their lives—and the relationships between them—are continually developing. Chapters 1, 2, 3, 11, and 12 are about adults' involvement. Chapters 4, 6, 7, 8, 9, and 10 focus primarily on social and emotional dimensions of bright kids' lives as they actively develop. Chapter 5 is about both kids and adults, because both have reason to be optimistic even while motivation to perform ebbs and flows.

Chapter 1: Recognizing Them

Identifying high ability can be challenging, and this chapter details many potential hurdles. Applying multiple criteria (not just performance on standardized tests) is now a mainstream perspective, as are casting a wide net and using group strategies to identify and nurture potential. This chapter explains the complexity of identification, including social and emotional implications of being identified, the variety of definitions of giftedness, and how behavior and verbal and social skills may affect selection for programs.

Chapter 2: Making Sense of Them

When we conduct conference sessions, we usually discuss some characteristics associated with high ability, such as heightened sensitivity and intensity. These characteristics affect how bright kids (and likely their parents) respond to life events, social interactions, and complex situations and changes at school and home. This chapter comes early in our book because it informs later chapters.

Chapter 3: Learning from Them

Professional preparation for interacting with bright kids often involves a top-down approach: learning *about* them from experts. Our approach as clinical professionals includes learning *from* them. This chapter offers detailed, practical guidance for listening and responding, since kids' internal world of stressors and perspectives is often inaccessible to adults or peers otherwise.

Chapter 4: Achieving and Underachieving

The gifted-education field often emphasizes performance—basing eligibility for selective programs on academic success; using high performers identified for programs as convenient subjects for studies of mental health, motivation to achieve, and career development; and giving little (usually negative) attention to underachievers who have high ability. Recent trends in the field include more research attention to underachievers, social and emotional development, qualitative research methods, and the whole child.

Chapter 5: Staying Optimistic About Underachievement

Adults often focus on the deficits of bright underachievers and on changing them. As clinical professionals, we stay alert to possible contributors to low academic performance, nonjudgmentally enter their world, and collaboratively work to improve their well-being, which in turn might affect their achievement. Findings in several Peterson studies about when academic performance declines, when it is resolved, and the role of development in both offer evidence that parents, guardians, teachers, directors, coaches, and other invested adults can be optimistic about better-than-expected outcomes.

Chapter 6: Living on the Edges, Twice-Exceptionally

Giftedness is one exceptionality. Any kind of disability—obvious or not—is another exceptionality. When high ability and disability occur together in a child or teen, the common descriptor is *twice-exceptional*. In this chapter, we and other experts offer explanation, strategies, and affirmation for this subpopulation in the high-ability world.

Chapter 7: Worrying

Anxiety is a common concern for children, teens, and adults who are intensely self-reflective, who have unusual emotional depth, and whose brains are hyperalert to contexts, change, loss, uncertainty, lack of control, perceived threat, self-expectations, expectations of others, and thoughts about the future. This chapter includes clinical perspectives about anxiety in bright children and teens.

Chapter 8: Fearing Failure: Perfectionism

Perfectionism, another common concern among highly capable people, may be obvious—or not. This chapter offers clinical and other information to help invested adults make sense of this phenomenon in bright kids, including distinguishing between a healthy striving for excellence and a debilitating fear of mistakes, of not meeting expectations, and of failure. Perfectionistic tendencies can prevent appreciation of the *process* when involved with projects—and preclude feelings of enjoyment and satisfaction along the way.

Chapter 9: Feeling, Struggling, Hiding

Highly able children and teens can hide distress expertly. They may be unwilling to risk their own or their family's positive image by talking about their distress. These kids are usually keenly aware of others' expectations of them, and they may actually have stressful, adult-like family roles because they are so capable. Adults might therefore be unaware of hidden struggles with eating, sleeping, doubt, shame, a learning disability, intense relationships, peer or adult bullying, or depression and thoughts of suicide. This chapter includes strategies for helping bright kids develop expressive language and cope with troubling situations.

Chapter 10: Coping with Adversity

The main focus of this chapter is resilience—being able to recover from difficult circumstances and move forward. It includes details and examples of personal qualities and circumstances that scholars and clinical professionals have associated with resilience, as well as perspectives from national experts on how to help kids develop resilience. It also explains the user-friendly concepts of grit, mindset, and brain-based parenting.

Chapter 11: Diagnosing and Misdiagnosing

Overexcitability, a concept associated with the intensities and sensitivities of high ability, can be psychomotor, intellectual, sensual, imaginational, and/or emotional. Associated behaviors may come to the attention of a counselor, school or clinical psychologist, or pediatrician. Overexcitabilities can be advantageous and viewed positively, or they can contribute to social and emotional challenges and even be misdiagnosed as psychological disorders. This chapter explores both misdiagnoses and "missed" diagnoses and emphasizes the importance of differentiating between diagnostic symptoms and characteristics associated with high ability.

Chapter 12: Parenting

This chapter looks at parenting from many angles. Parents are important models—for being kind to oneself, respecting others, embracing cultural diversity, exploring interests, playing, responding to mistakes, coping with stress, and enjoying the process of doing something challenging. What parents do affects how their bright children and teens view and respond to the world. Also discussed are parenting style, family hierarchy, creativity, and parental development.

HOW TO USE THIS BOOK

As we put this book together, we imagined it as a short course for adults wanting to build a base of knowledge for understanding their own bright kids, students, friends and relatives, employers or employees, business or therapy clients, or medical patients. In addition to this information, we have included suggestions and strategies for interacting effectively with high-ability children, teens, and older individuals. Detailed guidance about listening and responding, for example, can be put to use immediately. The information about characteristics, anxiety, perfectionism, resilience, underachievement, twice-exceptionality, and hidden distress might generate a meaningful, overdue discussion at home or with adult friends and acquaintances: "This is what I learned. Does it make sense to you? Tell me what you think of it."

The book is intended to be a rare resource for educators, clinical professionals, and parents and guardians. We can also imagine pediatricians and other medical professionals telling their patients or clients about our book or making it available for checkout when presenting issues might be explained by characteristics associated with high ability instead of or in addition to pathology. We can imagine teachers (whether in gifted or general education) doing the same, perhaps offering a descriptive flyer for parents, who might want their own copy. In one of our first conversations about this project, Dan pointed out that he hoped we could create a book to put into the hands of parents who bring their bright children and teens to him for counseling, to help them make sense of themselves and their kids.

Based on feedback after our many presentations and workshops at conferences and schools, what we have included in this book is not common knowledge. Bright individuals in our audiences routinely tell us afterward that they'd never heard anything that resonated so thoroughly with them. They tell us that we helped them make sense of themselves—and their kids, relatives, students, or clients. That is what we hope for you as you read this book.

Jean and Dan

Recognizing Them

TWO years ago, Justin was identified through state-mandated group testing as needing acceler-ated instruction; however, his rural school has no system in place for further assessment and for addressing his need for a more challenging curriculum. Now in his first year of middle school, he has become listless, anxious, and discouraged. One of his teachers recently expressed concerns about Justin's well-being to his parents, who then consulted with the school counselor, who in turn suggested that they search for mental health help in a nearby city. The counselor is unfamiliar with clinical professionals there, but she and Justin's parents plan to collaborate on a search for professional help. Unfortunately, none of them knows what to ask an agency as they pursue a good fit for this bright boy.

. . . .

A CLASSROOM teacher has referred Cristina, a third-grader, to the gifted-education teacher for possible participation in the program for high-ability students. English is an unfamiliar language for Cristina's mother, and her father grew up in a low-income urban US neighborhood. They have asked to meet with the classroom teacher not only because they need to give permission for an assessment, but also because they are not familiar with special programs. They wonder what the term *gifted* means, what the program involves, if they need to pay for Cristina's participation, and if she will no longer be with her friends in school.

. . . .

What do *high-ability* and *gifted* mean? What are the criteria for deciding who gets the *gifted* label? How is ability measured and giftedness identified? What should parents, teachers, counselors, and psychologists know to help them advocate for bright children and teens and, when warranted, seek services in and beyond the school district?

WHAT DO THE LABELS MEAN?

Language is powerful, and a label (or lack of it) can have life-altering impact during the school years. A label indicating high ability may not matter to some students or their families. But for others, this label may be the only ticket available for special opportunities, and it may affect how the students see themselves and how others see them.

The label *gifted,* when referring to students who have outstanding intellectual ability, is not universally embraced—even in the field of gifted education. Other common terms associated with high ability are *highly able, high capability, talented, gifted and talented, bright, high potential, advanced learner, profoundly intelligent,* and *highly intelligent.* When it seems necessary to distinguish points in the small uppermost section of the bell curve of intellectual ability, professionals use terms such as *exceptionally gifted, extreme ability, severely gifted,* and *profoundly gifted.* Giftedness researcher Françoys Gagné (2018) used the following terms for levels of intellectual or talent ability:

- mildly gifted: IQ greater than 120 (1 in 10 people)
- moderately gifted: IQ greater than 135 (1 in 100 people)
- highly gifted: IQ greater than 145 (1 in 1,000 people)
- exceptionally gifted: IQ greater than 155 (1 in 10,000 people)
- extremely gifted: IQ greater than 165 (1 in 100,000 people)

Clinical neuropsychologist John Wasserman (2007) gave different numbers for the final two categories, defining *exceptional ability* as having an IQ greater than 160 and *profoundly gifted* as having an IQ greater than 175. Labeling levels of giftedness is important because it may be used to determine the level of differentiation a child or teen needs in services. The higher the ability, the greater the social and emotional complexity, and the greater the need for differentiated academic and social and emotional curriculum.

However, a label can have social and emotional impact. For example, a child or teen, or their parent or guardian, might be uncomfortable if the term *gifted* is applied to their high level of measured intelligence. That label might have social costs, time costs, and pressure costs. In philosophical and political terms, with equity of opportunity in mind, the term can seem elitist. *Gifted* is usually not questioned when used to describe athletes, visual artists, musicians, and writers, but it is possible that educator language and tone, narrowly focused academic programs, and inappropriate identification practices do reflect elitism. For this reason, some professionals, school districts, and states have moved away from the term *gifted.* In this book we will usually use some form of the phrase *high*

> The higher the ability, the greater the social and emotional complexity, and the greater the need for differentiated academic and social and emotional curriculum.

ability when referring to standing out, having much more ability than average, and having high enough ability to warrant adjustments in school curriculum. We will use *gifted* when referring to gifted-education research findings and perspectives that apply that term. Our view is that high-ability students not only are complex individually, but also vary widely collectively. We embrace bright underachievers, bright kids with learning disabilities, bright individuals in complex home situations, and culturally and economically diverse gifted children and adolescents who are bright. Our language reflects that high ability—even intellectual brilliance—is not a narrow, precisely demarcated concept and can be found in any context.

Too often, only cognitive strengths and academic performance are considered when adults plan and deliver curriculum for highly able children and teens. Developmental tasks (related to identity, direction, relationships, and autonomy, for example) are basically universal, but how highly able kids *experience* developmental challenges differs from how other children and adolescents experience them. Our emphasis is therefore on social and emotional development, not just academic performance, and on the whole child, not just the child's performance.

WHO GETS THE LABEL?

School districts in the United States vary in their eligibility standards for special programs. The gifted-education field has long recommended some combination of the following for determining eligibility:

- a high score on a standardized (nationally field-tested and normed) assessment of cognitive or intellectual ability (memory; capacity to see connections, solve problems, learn) or achievement (knowledge accrued and/or applied), administered individually or in a group
- high classroom achievement and nomination by a teacher, parent, or self
- a portfolio of classroom or artistic products

When classroom achievement is the only eligibility criterion, the program offered is likely geared to high classroom *performers* only, regardless of *ability*. Because standardized group assessments often focus on math, science, and reading (and not on social studies, abstract thinking, creativity, spatial strengths, or writing), students identified by these assessments might be suited for advanced classes in one of those areas—but not necessarily in all three. In addition, some students might not be willing or able *at that time* to perform well in large-group testing; others can demonstrate accumulated knowledge in these tests in spite of a history of low classroom grades and in spite of circumstances. Individual ability (intelligence) testing is usually considered ideal for determining ability level, but conducting individual tests is labor-intensive and therefore expensive, making individual assessment access an economic equity issue.

To reduce the impact of socioeconomic status, lack of fluency in English, and learning differences on test results, nonverbal (visual) group-administered tests of cognitive ability are an option. Results of these tests strongly correlate with those of verbal tests, though nonverbal assessments may not identify highly verbal students or those with visual processing deficits. Tests that measure ability in multiple ways minimize these concerns.

> Students typically identified for gifted programs—as well as bright kids who are not identified—are highly idiosyncratic, varying greatly.

For determining program eligibility, a common cutoff score on a widely used standardized ability test is 130, above which is only a little more than 2 percent of the general population. But because special programs are meant to serve students who are so different from age peers in their community that the usual curriculum is not appropriate, school districts might use a different cutoff score: perhaps 120 (if only a small percentage are assessed to be above that, or if 15 to 20 percent are deemed to have high potential, and the program is geared to *developing* that potential) or 140 (if most students in a school or district are high-scoring, the general curriculum is geared to that level, and only extreme outliers need special curriculum). In typical gifted-education programs, students in Gagné's "mildly gifted" category are not likely to be involved because of the assumption that the regular curriculum, with modifications as warranted, is a good enough fit for them.

If IQ scores are extrapolated beyond the ceiling of what tests can actually measure, an IQ might be 190 or more in a profoundly gifted person, making the range of ability among those deemed gifted at least 60 IQ points—130 to 190 and beyond. Actually, new extended norms for the WISC-V, frequently used for individual IQ testing, now go up to 210 (Raiford et al. 2019). (The entire range of ability across 95 percent of a normal population is 60 IQ points—70 to 130—arguably smaller than the common range of students with the *gifted* label.) Therefore, students typically identified for gifted programs—as well as bright kids who are not identified—are highly idiosyncratic, varying greatly. When a scholar, teacher, or organization refers to "gifted children," "students with high potential," or "advanced learners," they are describing widely varying levels of ability with a single generic term. One-size-fits-all programs are not likely to address the needs and concerns of all students who need advanced-learner services.

QUANTITATIVE AND QUALITATIVE EVALUATION

Quantitative and qualitative evaluation used in tandem can help professionals understand the whole person, beyond academic performance. Evaluating ability quantitatively (statistically) is important—not only for identifying high ability when poor academic performance does not reflect it, but also to show differences in ability among high-ability kids. Quantitative evaluation of capability also allows comparisons among strengths and limitations in particular domains and measurement of cognitive changes over time. In contrast, qualitative evaluation may use interviews, observation, long-response

> We embrace the adage that what is measurable is not always important, and what is important is not always measurable.

questionnaires, and focus groups to assess whether or how mental and physical health, disabilities, or social functioning are affecting school experiences and demonstration of abilities. Teacher and parent questionnaires, portfolios of creative work or leadership, and real-world problem-solving may also be part of broad assessment.

When we work therapeutically with bright kids, qualitative approaches are essential. We are interested in their social and emotional concerns and development, their internal world, and their well-being. However, quantitative evaluation is crucial for understanding their academic, social, and emotional development and for guiding clinical intervention and school accommodation: educational evaluations (IQ test; achievement test in reading, writing, and math), psychoeducational evaluations (conducted by school and private psychologists—tests of ability and achievement; measures of mood, behavior, and visual, auditory, and social processing), and neuropsychological evaluations (not conducted in schools—psychoeducational testing, as listed above, and expanded measures of memory, attention, executive functioning, and visual, auditory, and social processing). Even with these several options, we need to have high tolerance for ambiguity and uncertainty as we explore how these kids make sense of their world.

In general, beyond assessment, we keep in mind that looking for a "cause" or one "reason" for a behavioral or emotional concern, and not considering themes in a child's or teen's language or patterns related to sleeping, eating, and studying, may mean that complex interactions are ignored. We may need multiple sessions before a sudden insight helps us make sense of a presenting issue.

We embrace the adage that what is measurable is not always important, and what is important is not always measurable. We sometimes frown when we hear bold statements about "the majority" in a research study, implying some unequivocal "truth" in education, likely to be cited by scholars for decades. The minority matter too. We have worked with many brilliant kids who do not fit majority findings about characteristics and behaviors. Unfortunately, their experiences may not be represented in textbooks and articles about high ability. It's important to remember that if, for example, 75 percent of bright kids behave in some way, 25 percent of bright kids do not. Both groups warrant attention. Clinically, we may work with that minority more than with the majority, but we know it is important not to assume that the majority have no counseling concerns, for example.

DETERMINING ELIGIBILITY

States, school districts, or schools decide the criteria for eligibility for special programming. Eligibility for gifted programs depends on what is considered high ability, what kind of assessment is used, whether the identification process casts a wide net to avoid missing a child with high potential, and perhaps even how many students an understaffed program can accommodate. Due to these variations, children might need scores of at least 120, 130, or 145 to be eligible. That means that in a school with a normal distribution of intelligence, approximately 10 percent, 2.25 percent, or 0.13 percent of the student body, respectively, would be identified as eligible. If a school or district is composed entirely of above-average or high-average students and program staffing is limited, it might use a higher cutoff score and identify a smaller percentage of students for a special program. Justification for that policy might be that teachers are already using curriculum and teaching methods appropriate for students with relatively high ability, and a program would address needs typical of students with even higher levels of ability. We believe that special programs, regardless of eligibility criteria, should not be limited to more-and-faster curriculum, but instead should also include experiences intended to broaden awareness and understanding in many fields—beyond the school curriculum.

A major problem with cutoff scores for determining eligibility is that no test is perfect. Each assessment for school services includes a range of measurement error, the difference between what a test score indicates and a student's actual knowledge and abilities. (News media, when reporting survey results, often refer to measurement error by saying "plus or minus X percentage points." However, parents, guardians, and teachers may not be aware that measurement error also applies to assessments of ability.) Committees should consider measurement error during the identification process. Scores on group-administered tests might underestimate ability if high-ability children and teens are anxious, ill, or preoccupied with family stress during testing; if they have learning, neurological, physical, or mental health issues warranting time or space accommodations that are not provided; or if the tests themselves have inherent bias. With individual face-to-face intelligence tests, a bright student may be uncomfortable with the size, voice, gender, or a behavior (for example, posture, type of eye contact, small talk at the outset) of the tester, or if the tester has biases that interfere with objectivity, test scores might not fall even within the error range. Regardless, testers should note, in any report, not only the error range, but also any observed anxiety or distractibility and the likelihood of underestimating or otherwise misassessing the child's ability.

MULTIPLE INTELLIGENCES

Not all schools and school districts limit identification of giftedness to intellectual ability. In the 1980s, Howard Gardner's theory of multiple intelligences (MI), which challenged traditional IQ-based views of intelligence, first gained media attention. Since 1999, he has identified eight relatively independent intelligences that process information differently: linguistic, logical-mathematical, musical, spatial, bodily/kinesthetic, interpersonal, intrapersonal, and naturalistic. Later, he and colleagues considered existential and pedagogical as additional intelligences. Many educators have appreciated Gardner's theory because it broadens how intellect can be defined and applied, but some scholars have criticized it as lacking empirical evidence (Gardner 2006). He has argued that his MI theory is based on "applied evidence," not "experimental evidence," and that experimental evidence is not appropriate for all theory development. Despite the controversy, Gardner has received numerous prestigious awards for his influential work.

In practice, schools usually assess only verbal and logical-mathematical intelligences to determine eligibility for programs, and programs (often limited to accelerated curricula) focus on those areas.

Exceptionality in other areas of intelligence—particularly social (interpersonal, leadership), self-knowledge (intrapersonal), and creativity—may not be considered. When programming is limited to verbal and math offerings—or even just math—bright students without strengths in those areas probably have a poor fit. Ideally programs fit the child, not vice versa, and offer curricula appropriate for students who excel in various areas of intelligence and address their needs. All bright students do not respond positively when limited to more-and-faster options. Jean observed, at length, impressive application of the MI theory in a program for high-ability children in an urban school and subsequently applied what she had learned when working clinically with bright children and teens.

Recognizing Potential

Casting a wide net (lowering the cutoff score or percentile ranking required for eligibility) helps professionals identify *potential*. Students can be clustered in each subject area according to level of intellectual strengths and/or achievement. Assessment happens not just once, and not just to determine basic eligibility, but periodically, allowing children to move to higher-level material when they're deemed ready to advance. This approach seems to suggest that high achievement and giftedness are synonymous, a specific perspective we do not embrace. However, we fully support the idea that widening the net to include students "with promise" offers them opportunities to learn and achieve academically. This kind of programming is different from programs with only more-and-faster academic work for students who are already achieving at a high level. The focus in this book on the whole child fits the wide-net view.

There is disagreement in the field about which scores qualify as "gifted"—and even whether a score is a useful indicator. Traditionalists believe that gifted people are the top 2 percent of the population in intellectual ability. Others espouse the top 5 percent. The former National Association for Gifted Children (NAGC) definition referred to the top 10 percent. In reality, giftedness is in the eye of the beholder. The concept of giftedness may reflect what is valued in a culture, and cultures differ in what they value. (See the "Cultural Values" section later in this chapter.) If the goals are informed decision-making and equity of opportunities, educators need to consider that policies and practices in US schools usually reflect the dominant US culture.

Dan participated on the most recent NAGC gifted definition task force, which crafted the following definition (National Association for Gifted Children 2019):

> Students with gifts and talents perform—or have the capability to perform—at higher levels compared to others of the same age, experience, and environment in one or more domains. They require modification(s) to their educational experience(s) to learn and realize their potential. Student with gifts and talents:
>
> • Come from all racial, ethnic, and cultural populations, as well as all economic strata.
>
> • Require sufficient access to appropriate learning opportunities to realize their potential.
>
> • Can have learning and processing disorders that require specialized intervention and accommodation.

- Need support and guidance to develop socially and emotionally as well as in their areas of talent.

- Require varied services based on their changing needs.

Note that this definition does not indicate a score. No score can account for the impact of personal circumstances on test performance and identification. This definition does promote equity in opportunity. It is the responsibility of educators to invest effort in identifying bright students whose health circumstances, cultural differences, or socioeconomic or family circumstances are interfering with classroom performance.

Highly capable underachievers may be no less gifted, by definition, than high academic achievers—endowed with exceptional *capacity* to learn, create, develop optimally and complexly, contribute, and produce. When they have family and/or school support, good fortune, good-fit relationships with teachers, and access to opportunities, underachievers can thrive. Educators owe them support and opportunities. But *thriving* and *giftedness* do not necessarily mean extraordinary academic achievement. Underachievers need special programs as much as high achievers do—and both can benefit from more differentiated programming than is usually offered in schools. Descriptors often listed as reflecting giftedness are these: curious, eager to learn, able to focus and learn quickly, drawn to deep learning in areas of interest; creative and insightful in thinking and problem-solving; able to recognize connections among disparate parts; self-motivated; keenly observant; and preferring older friends to age peers. Many of these fit positive stereotypes of "gifted kids." However, high intellectual ability is not always manifested in these ways, nor do they all describe all bright kids. Personality type, learning preferences, activity-level tendencies, and life circumstances vary greatly among bright kids and can affect how much they match the characteristics often found on checklists used during identification. Too many bright children and adolescents, some of them in high distress, cannot demonstrate these behaviors *at a particular time in their and their family's development*. Educators, counselors, and parents can work to broaden the range of qualities and circumstances they need to be alert to when their goal is to recognize high potential and high ability.

MANY ARE MISSED

Many highly able children and teens are not identified for special programming. Some simply do not fit common positive stereotypes associated with giftedness—well-behaved, compliant, highly verbal and articulate, voracious readers, socially skilled, culturally mainstream, high-achieving, with parents invested in their well-being—and therefore do not come to mind when teachers make referrals for further evaluation to determine eligibility. Highly able students with challenging behaviors may be not be referred by teachers for a second look because the latter believe that participation must be *deserved*—not necessarily *needed*. Some parents and guardians may have similar assumptions about what qualifies a child or teen for a special program.

Bright students may also be missed when only test scores and academic achievement determine eligibility, or when identification occurs before they arrive in the school district. A former school may not forward student records. Multiple teachers in a large middle school may have few opportunities to discuss students they have in common. Parents and guardians with heavy work schedules may not be able to schedule a meeting with a teacher to advocate for their child. Students who are English language learners probably cannot yet show their ability on verbal assessments or in the classroom. Twice-exceptional (2e) students (cognitive giftedness as one exceptionality; one or more emotional, behavioral, developmental, physical, speech-language, or learning disabilities as a second exceptionality) also may not perform well in those areas, declining at each new school level, especially when learning preferences fit poorly with a teacher. Bright students who live in low-income households, who are homeless, or who live in underresourced or remote areas may not have had opportunities for intellectual enrichment outside of school comparable to those of their middle- and upper-income peers.

> Having abilities affirmed, regardless of academic performance level and stage of development, is important.

Racial or cultural bias in teachers, school administrators, test administrators, and tests themselves may have an impact on identification of high ability. Finally, traumatic experiences such as domestic or community violence, sexual or other physical abuse, emotional abuse, a natural disaster, a life-threatening illness or accident, or death of a loved one can affect school attendance and behavior, relationships with teachers and peers, and motivation to achieve academically—any of which may affect if and how ability is demonstrated.

Not being identified for a program can negatively affect bright children. They might not be able to enroll in some or any advanced classes, which can limit their access to intellectual peers and peers who share their interests. They may miss important interaction that informs them about themselves and helps them develop social skills. If the gate is closed during the only year formal identification is conducted, or if they cannot perform well in a narrowly conceptualized program that is the only option available, they may not have a second chance.

Having abilities affirmed, regardless of academic performance level and stage of development, is important. Capable but underachieving students need to have regular contact with their intellectual peers in activities and classes. As they continue to develop, their achievement may improve (see chapter 5). When students miss opportunities to interact with those peers and have their exceptional ability validated, their confidence in their intellectual strengths might erode.

CULTURAL VALUES

Fundamentally, giftedness is in the eye of the beholder. Cultures differ in what they value, and how a culture responds to the idea of giftedness may reflect what is valued in that culture. Cultural values may prevent students from eagerly showing what they know in the classroom. In Jean's dissertation study of Midwestern middle school teachers' language as they nominated students for a program for gifted students, the teachers justified their nominations by referring to a wide array of perceived "gifted behaviors," such as verbal skills and assertiveness, organization, knowledge, production, eagerness to learn, willingness to contribute to class discussion and demonstrate knowledge publicly, competitiveness, high academic achievement, and perfection. These behaviors suggest that *individual, competitive, conspicuous achievement* is valued in mainstream US culture.

The five main themes in the teachers' nomination language are listed below in order from most to least mentioned. Unexpectedly, they included aspects of social and emotional development and did not include intellectual ability:

- behavior (good behavior arguing for inclusion, bad behavior for exclusion)
- verbal ability and assertiveness
- family status
- work ethic
- social skills

When the five themes listed above serve as informal criteria for identification, they might exclude bright children like the following:

- kids with noncompliant, disruptive behavior or poor social skills
- shy, anxious kids
- kids with advanced abilities or exceptional potential in nonverbal areas (such as computer graphics, design, technology, music composition, computer programming, or creative engineering)
- kids with troubled lives who are not engaged in school activities and are not focused on academics
- kids whose work ethic is directed at babysitting younger siblings, preparing meals, doing laundry, helping with a family business, or having paid employment to help support the family
- kids who do not have an easy relationship with teachers, peers, and administrators
- kids whose parents are not involved at school, are not respected in the community, or have poor social skills

In a follow-up study, during which Jean immersed herself in five US communities (Black, Native American, Latinx, recent Southeast Asian immigrants, and low-income White communities), adults nominated "the most gifted" people they had known. These adults mentioned none of the behaviors mentioned by teachers in Jean's dissertation study. Instead, the themes that emerged were humility, "not standing out," helping the community, arts as expression (not performance), listening and nurturing, nonbookish learning, and wisdom (not knowledge).

Jean concluded that teachers may be looking for "gifted behaviors" that are not valued or promoted in some cultures—and therefore are not demonstrated in the classroom. Kids and parents may not realize that teachers are looking for verbal assertiveness and active class participation. Jean also concluded that teachers are likely to identify kids who resemble the teachers in behavior, who affirm them as teachers, and who show eagerness to learn from them.

The minority-culture parents were not likely to advocate for special services for their high-ability children, in some cases because they trusted that teachers would recognize their children's ability and make sure they were included in programs—without parental input. Findings in these two studies are reminders that for students who might not surface through group-administered standardized tests, teacher-child and peer-to-peer interactions matter when teachers are asked to make referrals for special services for bright kids. Kids who are not referred are not likely to be looked at further (that is, through school records or teacher, parent, or peer checklists).

POINTS TO PONDER

- Level of ability matters; it guides differentiation of curriculum and services.
- Measurement error might not be considered during identification.
- Not all bright kids are identified; many are missed.
- Types of students identified reflect the qualifying criteria and perhaps the type of program offered.
- Not all bright students achieve well in school.
- Cultural values may inhibit showing or recognizing advanced abilities.

Making Sense of Them

THROUGHOUT elementary school, Liesl's teachers had recognized her brilliance. Each in turn eventually checked school records and confirmed Liesl's off-the-charts ability. Each consulted with her previous teachers to learn how they had helped Liesl avoid explosive outbursts, which thwarted relationships and disrupted discussions. In elementary school, her main teachers, who had full-day contact with Liesl on most days, were able to chat quietly with her now and then, express interest in her thoughts, and ask about what she was drawing or painting at home. Most of these teachers learned to value her wry humor, writing skills, and precocious insights.

But that precarious balance was upset when Liesl entered middle school and had only one class period daily with each teacher. Liesl quickly earned a reputation as a prickly, bossy, impatient student in the classroom, at lunch, during physical education, and during chorus practices. At the first parent-teacher conference, her bright, soft-spoken parents were alarmed when each teacher seemed to struggle to make positive comments. Because Liesl was earning only high average marks, the teachers appeared unable to see beyond her negative behaviors. They had not consulted with the school psychologist or counselor to see if information in her school records might help them understand this complicated girl.

. . . .

Some parents and guardians are concerned, disturbed, or even scared when they realize that their children's high intellectual ability makes them quite different from other children. These parents may have questions: *Someone mentioned that my kid might be gifted—what does that mean? What do I do now? How different is she? Is this differentness going to be a problem for him? What will her life be like? What will he need? Are there other kids like her? Why do people look at me funny when I tell them what he's doing? Who can help me make sense of him? What about when she's in school? Will she ever fit in? Will he ever have peers he can relate to? Will she be okay? How will my life change? Why am I feeling so unsettled? Is there anyone who can answer my questions?* Liesl's parents and her elementary-school teachers collaborated enough to

> High ability can be both strength and vulnerability, asset and burden, advantage and disadvantage. It affects all areas of life, including how kids respond to developmental challenges.

answer some of these questions, but the transition to a larger school, with multiple teachers arrayed across a compartmentalized curriculum, brought discrepancies among cognitive, social, and emotional development sharply into view.

Other parents and guardians feel happy and proud about their children's high ability. When their toddler speaks in paragraphs or can manipulate toys, markers, and utensils precociously, they notice, but are not concerned. Perhaps other children in their social world are highly able too. Exceptional ability is normal there. They have few questions or concerns—at least for a while. In the meantime, they enjoy an easy repartee with their child, their child's sense of humor, the verbal or spatial games they can play together, or the creativity they observe in their child.

Regardless of the scenario, parents can benefit from information that helps them make sense of their children—and probably themselves. Acorns don't fall far from their trees, after all. Bright kids often have bright parents. However, their specific strengths and abilities may differ.

In this chapter we provide information about bright kids with the hope that invested adults will not be awed by these children and teens or intimidated by them, since neither of those responses is likely to be helpful in generating a trusting relationship. Instead, we hope adults will embrace the idea that high-ability children and teens are whole, complex people—with strengths, limitations, developmental challenges, concerns, and doubts—who need support and nurturing. Some of these kids fit common positive stereotypes of giftedness; some do not. We believe, based on our interactions with both, that exceptional intelligence can actually put them at risk for poor personal and educational outcomes, regardless of achievement level, because it can exacerbate struggles during personal and family transitions.

Learning about characteristics associated with high ability can help bright children and teens make sense of themselves. Such awareness in adults can similarly help them make sense of high-ability kids. The characteristics discussed in the rest of this chapter can all be assets in developing talent, interests, insights, and products—but they can also negatively affect relationships at home, at school, and elsewhere.

THE ASSET–BURDEN PARADOX

High ability can be both strength and vulnerability, asset and burden, advantage and disadvantage. It affects all areas of life, including how kids respond to developmental challenges.

High intelligence can help with problem-solving, making sense of situations, feeling in control, focusing in the classroom, and communicating with teachers and others in authority. Intelligence is also usually viewed as contributing to resilience, helping children and teens not only survive adversity, but gain perspective and strength from it. High ability can help students with learning disabilities compensate for them. In counseling, the assets of high ability can help bright kids articulate and address the associated burdens.

ASSETS AND BURDENS: A CLINICAL EXAMPLE

In a longitudinal study of a gifted young woman (from age fifteen through thirty) who struggled with the complex aftermath of multiple traumas, Jean (Peterson 2012, 2014) found symptoms of post-traumatic stress disorder (PTSD) and challenges related to developmental tasks (identity, direction, relationships, and autonomy). Jean created a table listing the young woman's assets and burdens related to high ability and found that the two lists were nearly equal.

Assets	Burdens
• She had positive relationships with teachers.	• She had adultlike roles at home.
• She knew how to access resources.	• Her parents were uncomfortable with her abilities.
• She could monitor her emotions and behaviors.	• Because of her impressive strengths, her parents discounted her needs and concerns.
• She knew how to protect and advocate for herself.	• She needed, and was capable of, extreme involvement in activities to help her feel control.
• She was able to express herself clearly and directly.	• She felt intense emotional pain.
• She could apply what she learned from self-help books.	• Her colleagues viewed her as "too successful" in her first professional job.
	• Others' needs emotionally drained her.

Eventually, the young woman summarized how she experienced the asset-burden paradox. First, she mentioned the burdens: Others assumed she was fine, had advantages, needed to be taught hard lessons, and did not need help. Her mother did not know how to parent a bright, intense, conflicted, verbally adept child. Her most painful and unsettling emotional experiences were exacerbated by characteristics of giftedness, such as intensity and heightened sensitivity.

She also recognized her assets. Intensities pushed her to try to stop her internal upheaval, to learn about what she was experiencing, to make sense of people, to invest in developing a career, and to dive into parenting her children after initially worrying that she had had poor parenting models during childhood and adolescence. She questioned what was real and what was unreal. She recognized when she misread situations. She worked hard to face her fears. She recognized epiphanies, which helped her frame her experiences. She sought therapy when she needed it. She said the assets of high ability propelled her forward.

High ability comes with potential burdens. One is the weight of high—perhaps even extreme—expectations, from both self and others. Bright kids may have adultlike roles at home, such as being in charge of food preparation and laundry, being an adult's confidant, or having inappropriately heavy responsibility during complex family decision-making. Being able to control emotions and focus can be advantageous in the classroom, but putting a lid on feelings may be detrimental to overall well-being. An active mind may not rest easily and might interfere with sleep. Age peers may not know how to interact with bright, intense kids, and the latter may feel isolated or rejected.

Adults may also have negative feelings about highly able kids. They may refer to them as being "too much"—too intense, too emotional, too insistent, too busy, too preoccupied, too fussy, too successful. They may make such comments to the kids directly. If teachers believe that high ability means not having family, social, or academic problems, they might not recognize bullying, dangerous stress levels, and grief in response to change and loss in bright students. Adults may also assume that development is less challenging for bright kids, missing the reality that growing up is simply a *different kind* of struggle for them. Adults may discount concerns of bright children and teens. In addition, both positive and negative biases can interfere with compassionate support. Positive biases can prevent adults from recognizing needs, and negative biases can generate hostility. Unconscious biases may prompt competitive humor and unwelcome repartee about knowledge that can leave little or no space for nurturing. Attitudes and judgments about high performers, low performers, and their parents may also create barriers.

In a study of negative life events experienced by gifted kids and their families during the K–12 school years, "overinvolvement" in activities was a common thread. Having "no life outside of school" was another (Peterson, Duncan, and Canady 2009). Other themes reflected areas not often discussed as burdensome in connection with high ability:

- hidden, silent sensitivity
- feeling different; experiencing ridicule, isolation, and hostility, including from "resentful" teachers
- high ability not necessarily equated with advanced maturity, though others think it is
- apathy; not caring about school as much as teachers and parents think
- family stress, with school being the "safe haven"
- "trying too hard"
- not wanting to be singled out for having high ability

The burdens of high ability might bring bright kids to counseling, and the assets of high ability may help them make good use of counseling to resolve challenging problems. Unfortunately, counselors are unlikely to have had even brief training specifically related to bright kids, according to a study of accredited programs (Peterson and Wachter Morris 2010).

Families, teachers, and other advocates can provide school and community counselors with resources about the social and emotional development of students with high ability.

Clinically, appealing to bright students' cognitive strengths, we have found that acknowledging the asset-burden paradox and providing information about characteristics associated with high ability can help these students make sense of uncomfortable emotions and troubling behaviors. They typically embrace the concept quickly and appreciate opportunities to discuss high ability in a new way—different from the common focus on performance and achievement.

A HIGHLY IDIOSYNCRATIC POPULATION

Children and teens with high ability are idiosyncratic, each of them unique in how abilities are demonstrated and how characteristics apply. The spectrum of giftedness is broad and complicated. It includes bright kids whose capable minds are not a burden and for whom high expectations and involvement in school and community activities are comfortable. High-ability children and teens with disabilities are also in that broad range, as are profoundly or extremely gifted kids. The strengths, limitations, and consequent stressors for each may be burdensome and distressing. At the upper levels of intellectual ability, kids may have access to few, if any, mind-mates in their school or community. Such differentness has social and emotional implications, of course.

Inappropriate generalizations about high-ability students are common even at gifted-education conferences. Some examples are that gifted kids are highly verbal, are likely to have meltdowns, don't sleep well, and are healthy emotionally. Such statements should be heard and read critically. Nonetheless, clinical professionals and scholars who explore social and emotional development of bright kids do have helpful insights to offer, and the rest of this chapter includes some of them.

The above observations can help bright, complicated children and teens make sense of themselves and can provoke thought and self-reflection in involved adults. Understanding and acknowledging these perspectives may be crucial to addressing school-related problems and concerns. Many such problems have a social, relational aspect. Many reflect emotional struggles as well. Left unaddressed, problems may grow. Likewise, if academic problems related to intellectual ability are not addressed, social and emotional concerns may appear.

UNIVERSAL DEVELOPMENTAL TASKS, EXPERIENCED DIFFERENTLY

The developmental tasks of bright kids are essentially the same as those of their age peers, regardless of culture. They move toward identity, a sense of self. They develop interests, find career direction, and move toward adult roles. They learn about living in relationship with others—eventually experiencing culturally appropriate mature relationships. They figure out how to be separate from, but still connected with, parents and family. They ponder gender identity, gender roles, and sexuality. They move toward competence and confidence. The details of these developmental tasks and accomplishments look different across cultures, but the basic *tasks* are similar. Human development varies in tempo, of course, and individuals may feel "stuck" along the way. Chapters 4 and 9 discuss this phenomenon.

> The developmental tasks of bright kids are essentially the same as those of their age peers, regardless of culture.

Developmental psychologists, experts in the field of gifted education, and mental health professionals who have worked with bright, complicated children and teens have concluded that several social and emotional characteristics—in addition to remarkable cognitive strengths and agility—distinguish these kids from most of their age peers. Awareness of these characteristics can help parents, guardians, teachers, coaches, directors, and mentors make sense of the behaviors and emotions they see in high-ability kids. What distinguishes bright kids from their peers besides ability? The characteristics we describe next *may exacerbate challenges related to developmental tasks.*

Heightened Sensitivity and Intensity

According to Sal Mendaglio (2007), the rapid information processing associated with intellectual giftedness contributes to heightened, multifaceted sensitivity. Thinking more means feeling more, being more self-critical, being more emotionally intense and changeable, and experiencing reality differently and more intensely than most other people. People with intellectual strengths are likely to be quite aware of their emotional states and perspectives. However, Mendaglio cautions against thinking of sensitivity and intensity narrowly, simply as dramatic emotional expression, and instead as reflecting a highly active brain. He also notes that how someone is socialized affects whether and how much they communicate their sensitivity.

One way in which sensitivity manifests in some high-ability kids is depression. James Webb (2013), a respected theorist in the gifted-education field, connected existential depression with bright students' struggles to find meaning. Children and adolescents with high ability are aware of how the world could and should be (fair, trustworthy and predictable, with adults as capable problem-solvers). When they see inconsistencies and consider complex questions, their idealism, sensitivity, and concerns about fairness may lead to disillusionment and despair.

Intensity, felt internally and perhaps evident externally, is also associated with high ability. Susan Daniels and Michael Piechowski (2009) wrote that passionate interests, intense emotions, and intense responses to life events, disorder, stress, or competition can affect family life, appetite, sleep, relationships with teachers and peers, and well-being. Intensity can turn inward in the form of self-deprecation. It might also explode outward.

Intensity and sensitivity can be strengths, potentially channeled toward productivity and success. But how others view and respond to intensity and sensitivity affects how exceptional children and teens view themselves. Extreme sensitivity to sensory stimuli, such as visual images, sounds, textures, and smells, may contribute to discomfort at home; in high-texture, stimulus-rich classrooms; in activities both indoors or outdoors; and in employment. Intensity and sensitivity can affect even normal developmental transitions, such as entering kinder-garten, experiencing puberty, being away from family overnight for the first time, or leaving for college, which may exacerbate the challenges of these experiences. Meanwhile, some adults might believe that bright kids "shouldn't have these problems."

Unfortunately, sensitivity reflected in tantrums, meltdowns, anxiety, anger, or hyper-sensitive responses to sensory stimuli may be misunderstood, dismissed as simply weird, or in other ways not taken seriously. Not all bright, talented children and teens are confi-dent. In the study of negative life events mentioned on page 22, when bright students in their final year of high school were asked about "hindrances to success," they mentioned shyness, social awkwardness, feeling inferior, fear of new situations, lack of confidence, self-consciousness, perfectionism, sensitivity to criticism, and being too trusting. Findings also suggested that intensity may lead to increasingly high stress during the school years, extreme competitiveness, and investing in too many activities. In addition, bright children and teens with high moral development and sensitivity may be intensely affected by stories of social injustice in the news (Peterson, Duncan, and Canady 2009).

Overexcitabilities

Michael Piechowski (2013) brought the concept of overexcitabilities (OEs, introduced earlier by Kazimierz Dabrowski) to the gifted-education field. *OEs* refers to intense experiencing in intellectual, sensual, imaginational, emotional, or psychomotor arenas: passionate interests, empathic connections to others, a strong sense of justice and fairness, creativity, strong emotional connections, sensitive responses to sensory stimuli, and constant move-ment. OEs can be positive (for example, fantasy, heightened emotional responses, intense need to understand) and negative (for example, inhibition, anxiety, extreme feelings, nervousness, tics, internal tension, strong social and emotional memories).

Asynchronous Development

The high ability of bright children and teens does not always catch the attention of coun-selors. If it does, it may be because high intelligence coexists with developmental delays, disruptive behavior, or low academic performance. Another possibility is asynchronous development, that is, precociously developed intellectual ability or talent that is out of sync with average or below-average social and emotional development (Silverman 2013). As the level of cognitive ability increases, the amount of asynchrony often also increases. When

> Being different and feeling different from most others their age can be uncomfortable.

cognitive, social, and emotional development are equally developed, those aspects are in sync. In contrast, uneven development can contribute to bright kids being out of sync with age-related expectations and feeling out of sync with age peers—that is, dyssynchrony (Silverman 2013). Being different and feeling different from most others their age can be uncomfortable. Adults can acknowledge and validate this experience and help bright, sensitive kids accept their differentness, learn how to navigate the culture of their age peers, and thrive in it despite an uneasy fit with it.

Clinical professionals and parents may see interpersonal challenges that result from asynchrony, especially with ability at extreme levels. These challenges include not having mind-mates; having heavy adult-level roles and responsibilities at home, at school, or at work; and not being able to make sense of emotions in various situations. Teachers and counselors may notice large gaps between high academic achievement, impressive vocabulary, and advanced critical thinking on one hand and inability to articulate emotions, cope with challenges, and understand social interactions on the other. Low classroom achievers with high ability may also struggle with being out of sync, of course.

Multipotentiality

Multipotentiality refers to having two or more exceptional talents or strong areas of interest, each being a reasonable option for a promising career path. As clinicians, we see high-ability, multitalented kids who are unsettled about having so many choices, and their distress can complicate decision-making about career direction, college type and location, and major. Multipotentiality may actually raise the specter of loss, because making a choice requires leaving other options behind.

Misdiagnosis and Missed Diagnoses

A final area of concern related to high ability is that its characteristics, because they resemble symptoms of various emotional and behavioral disorders and learning disabilities, may be misdiagnosed as pathology. *Misdiagnosis* can also occur when intellect is not considered during assessment and therapy (Webb et al. 2016). Because giftedness is not a clinical diagnosis, it is not included in the diagnostic manuals. Clinical professionals who are not familiar with literature related to giftedness may therefore not consider the interaction between high ability and school contexts. Behaviors reflecting asynchronous development, a poor fit with an inappropriate program, or intense reactions to stimuli can be misunderstood. Inappropriate diagnostic labels may be applied, affecting sense of self. Great strengths may then be ignored.

On the other hand, high-ability individuals can have disorders that are unrecognized—in other words, *missed diagnoses*. Diagnosable disorders, such as obsessive-compulsive disorder (OCD), anxiety, and various kinds of depression, can be masked by the ability to compensate for them. Odd behaviors may be viewed simply as typical of high-ability kids and therefore dismissed as being of no concern. (See chapter 11 for more information.)

POINTS TO PONDER

- Bright kids, like all kids, have both strengths and limitations. It's okay to have limitations.

- Being bright is both an asset and a burden.

- High-ability kids face the same developmental tasks as anyone else, but often *experience* them differently.

- Certain characteristics are associated with high ability.

- Asynchronous development can mean having advanced cognitive abilities but being less developed in other areas.

- Being so different from most others their age can be uncomfortable for bright children and teens.

- When bright kids can connect the dots and make sense of themselves, they feel less strange.

Learning from Them

COLE, thirteen, who attends a large middle school, has become a target of bullying by a classmate with a posse—in the hallway, in the locker room after soccer practice, in the lunchroom, and recently, when he walks home. Teachers have referred to him as "shy and very bright" since kindergarten. He misses his good friend from elementary school, whose family moved to a neighborhood served by a different middle school. Cole believes he can't talk with his father about the bullying, but he mentioned it to his mother a few days ago. She is also a shy person, but she knows she should talk with Cole's adviser, soccer coach, and principal about the bullying. She does not have confidence in her ability to talk with any of them, especially because she has heard how intimidating they all are. She is grateful that Cole told her about the problem and wishes she had resources that would help her approach people in authority and practice assertiveness with Cole so that he might be able to self-advocate with teachers.

Caring adults might hesitate to initiate conversation with kids. Adults can be intimidated by the thought that they need to be animated and stimulating in conversations if they are to compete with kids' usual fare of games, texting, social media, and other visual stimuli. With bright kids, adults might feel extra pressure to be engaging. Some might also fear that if they do make contact, they will hear about something they will need to "fix." Some may think the only way to talk with kids is to give advice or to ask many questions to show interest. These assumptions are unfortunate. They may not only prevent conversations but also contribute to missed opportunities to gain insights about the internal world of kids.

This chapter offers guidance for talking with kids—especially bright kids. It is safe to assume that most children and teens welcome an adult's interest in talking with them. Because of available technology and more classwork being done online, they may have few face-to-face conversations in which eyes, mouth, facial expressions, posture, and words all matter. Here we draw on our training and clinical experiences with bright kids to share basic concepts related to listening and responding that work in a wide variety of contexts. Listening skills improve with practice. When adults regularly apply the guidelines we have included, and self-reflect afterward about what they did, they may be able to connect more often and more comfortably with children and teens themselves and help the kids interact with peers more smoothly and meaningfully as well. Such conversations are worth the required investment, and both kids and adults are likely to develop skills through them.

PAYING ATTENTION

Bright children and adolescents, like all kids, have social and emotional concerns. Growing up is a complicated process for anyone. But kids whose intellectual ability and talent make them different from most age peers can feel abnormal, lonely, angry, frustrated, overwhelmed, sad, and scared. Adults cannot know about these concerns unless the kids tell them.

Based on our various experiences with them, we can attest that high-ability children and adolescents can hide their concerns expertly—even when in great distress. Peers, teachers, or parents might not suspect intense concerns, even when they see disruptive behavior, a sad face, withdrawal from peers, low energy, or lack of motivation for classroom work. Difficulties may be related to or exacerbated by the characteristics of high ability discussed in chapter 2. When opportunities to engage bright, sensitive kids present themselves, good listening is important.

GIVING UP SOME CONTROL

Adults who are good listeners have learned to give away some control. They need to be quiet if they are genuinely interested in the well-being and social and emotional development of bright, sensitive kids. Not being directive and not being in charge may be difficult for teachers. They may feel anxious when they are "just listening," because that means they have less control than when they are managing a classroom and organizing and delivering curriculum. Parents and guardians who take their child-rearing responsibilities seriously often have an impulse to advise and instruct. Coaches may be so absorbed in directing talent development that it doesn't occur to them to change the mode of interaction—to listen more than they speak and demonstrate.

Teachers may think the best approach to connecting with a student is to ask questions. But questions in conversation usually reflect the questioner's agenda, interests, and curiosity, not the student's.

Changing the mode—becoming the learner, not the parent, teacher, or guide—is basic to giving up control. High-ability children and teens can indeed teach adults about what they experience and how they experience it—if the adults know when and how to listen.

Effective listening means being open to someone else's agenda—*facilitating* conversation without controlling it. Teachers may think the best approach to connecting with a student is to ask questions. But questions in conversation usually reflect the questioner's agenda, interests, and curiosity, not the student's. Parents may have a similar impulse, intending to show interest by asking questions. But they cannot know which questions need to be asked—and how they should be asked. Peppering kids with questions, regardless of the kind or amount, is unlikely to open a window to their complex world. Actually, as explained later in this chapter, entire conversations are possible without questions.

NOT COMMUNICATING AS PEERS

When adults interact with children and adolescents, they are not communicating as peers. They are also neither friends nor confidants. Peers talk as relative equals. In conversations between adults and children, adults have the power—the power of age, hierarchy, life experience, and perhaps even size.

When they are quiet and listen attentively to kids, adults *give away some power* and become learners. That role change can empower the younger person. When adults don't dominate or control the interaction, unexpected conversation strands may appear. When an adult assumes a "one-down" posture (being *taught* by the child or teen) instead of a "one-up" posture (*teaching*, directing the young person), kids may invite the adult in.

Being quiet and listening requires effort and focus. Being preoccupied with fixing, advising, telling, or steering usually precludes good listening. In contrast, listening without criticizing, judging, or needing to fix situations; staying poised and not anxious (no matter what kids say); and standing solidly with them during a stressful time may encourage them to talk.

MAKING PERSONAL CONNECTIONS

Most counselors and other clinical professionals believe that the therapeutic relationship may be the most important element in personal growth, resolving concerns, problem-solving, and exploring future directions. We believe this view also applies to kids' relationships with mentors, teachers, parents, grandparents, and other invested adults. Thomas Hébert's (1995, 2001, 2018) interview-based studies of troubled young people who were eventually successful; participants' sustained investment in Jean's (2002) four-year study of bright,

When kids perceive that an adult cares, is interested in them individually, and knows them to some extent, this relationship may be a crucial safe harbor when the sea is rough.

sensitive teens at high risk for poor educational and personal outcomes; and Dan's clinical experiences with school-age clients have shown that when kids perceive that an adult cares, is interested in them individually, and knows them to some extent, this relationship may be a crucial safe harbor when the sea is rough.

Teachers can begin to make purposeful personal connections through small talk before a class begins, while monitoring a hallway, standing at the classroom door, or walking around the classroom while students are settling in. They might initiate a brief interaction with one of the following: "How's your day going?" "Are you okay sitting in the back?" "Looks like we'll have rain the rest of the day. Do you have to be out in it after school?" "I'm curious—have you always lived here?" "I saw you in the chorus at that great program last night." Some of these low-stakes questions or comments are answerable with *yes* or *no*, but after a few days of these, a longer conversation might happen. Showing interest in a student with an expectant facial expression is a key element. Not demanding a conversation may help develop trust. A warm smile and a head nod to a student walking by can do the same. If a personal crisis has scared a student, or if a stressful situation arises in the future, the student might come to the teacher for help because the teacher seems interested and nice.

Similar noninvasive questions and comments can work well for parents and guardians. They might ask, "How was your day today?" "I've been wondering if the thunderstorm/snow/tornado warning affected the kids." "Who was your best teacher today?" On another day, parents might ask, "I was trying to imagine you in your school building during the day. Which parts of the building do you spend time in?" In another conversation, they might ask about emotions: "Where in the building do you feel the most stress? Where (or when) did you feel best today?" In yet another conversation, location could be the focus: "What would I see in the lunchroom?" "What would I see in the hallways (or bus area after school)?" "How would you describe the atmosphere of your school (or classroom)?"

DEVELOPING SKILLS FOR LISTENING AND RESPONDING
Questions and Statements

Closed questions (answerable with *yes* or *no*) do not usually generate conversation. Open-ended questions are more likely to lead to elaboration and explanation. They often begin with the words *what, how, when,* and *what kind of,* as in the following:

- "How do you know when your dad is paying attention to you?"
- "What do you understand about divorce?"
- "What led to the fight with your friend?"
- "When are you likely to ask a teacher for what you need?"
- "When do you feel comfortable (or uncomfortable) at home?"
- "How are you different this year, compared with last year?"
- "What kinds of comments upset you most?"
- "What do you wish teachers (or parents, principal, or peers) understood about you?"

Responses to open-ended questions need more than just a few words. Saying "Tell me more about that" or "Help me understand what you meant by that" also invites detail.

It's important to remember that questions can control a conversation, preventing a person who needs to talk (to someone who will "just listen") from expressing what needs to be said. However, a listener may ask questions simply out of curiosity, as listeners do in peer-to-peer conversations. When a crisis is being described, it makes sense for listeners to ask for details to determine the level of urgency. In such situations, remembering the words that begin open-ended questions can lead to detailed, informative responses.

In contrast, productive conversations can be generated entirely with *statements* (instead of questions) in response to comments, such as these:

- "Sounds as if you've been struggling with your brother lately."
- "I can hear that you're frustrated (or upset, sad, annoyed, desperate, confused, irritated, angry, scared, stressed, or really tired)."
- "So you're planning to arrange to talk with your friend (or dad, mom, or grandma) about this."
- "That must've been scary."
- "I can see why you're feeling so overwhelmed lately."
- "That sounds like a good plan."
- "I predict that your stress level will go down a little if you follow your plan."
- "What you just described is a good example of social intelligence and wisdom."
- "That's an important insight."
- "That sounds complicated."
- "You obviously were quite concerned."
- "Relationships can be confusing."
- "It makes sense that you're angry. That's a big, very normal feeling. I'm glad you recognize it."

The statements above are validators. These responses assure speakers that they are being heard. They punctuate what speakers say. They do not evaluate or judge. Some statements validate strengths. Others name emotions, which may be difficult to talk about. Naming emotions helps kids develop expressive language. Statements and questions about emotions, like the following, can provoke self-reflection and generate helpful information:

- "What does stress feel like for you?"
- "Tell me more about 'scary.'"

- "Help me understand how often you feel that kind of fear."
- "How do you usually manage sad feelings?"
- "How do you usually show your frustration?"
- "If you were really angry right now, how would I know?"

A nonjudgmental attitude is key. Emotions are not "bad" or "good." Feelings just *are*. They can become less unsettling and uncomfortable when they are expressed, discussed, and sorted out.

Finally, statements suggesting personal strengths are usually helpful if they are credible, based on observation or on information the child has shared:

- "You watch people carefully—you're a good observer."
- "I'm confident you'll do what you need to when you're ready."
- "I've seen that you're able to be assertive when you need to be and get what you need."
- "I'm glad you can imagine a future that's different."
- "I've seen you be kind and helpful to other kids."
- "You're a good problem-solver for your sisters and brother."
- "You're able to bounce back, and I'm confident that you will do that again. But I know you're disappointed and hurting now."
- "You're a survivor."
- "You're here today—in spite of everything."

Communicating Nonverbally

There are many ways adults can enter a child's or teen's world gently, without judgment. Physical, nonverbal aspects of communication are fundamental. For example, an open posture helps invite interaction—arms and legs not crossed; leaning slightly forward, not back; not encroaching on personal space. Responsive facial expressions communicate interest, warmth, and empathy, which are important for building trust and rapport. Eye contact is appropriate if it feels safe to the

> A nonjudgmental attitude is key. Emotions are not "bad" or "good." Feelings just *are*.

younger person. However, adults should be aware that lack of eye contact from children and teens may not reflect disrespect, lack of confidence, or shame. If they give eye contact readily, an adult probably doesn't need to wonder why. However, if the eyes are directed downward, we discourage adults in a helping, supportive role from challenging that. They might instead consider why insisting on direct eye contact might preclude a beneficial relationship. We recognize that, depending on context, cultural background, and parents' modeling, probation officers, school administrators, and even parents may believe that demanding eye contact, including with a shaming tone, is essential to discouraging negative behavior. We disagree—and offer some alternative perspectives here.

Disabilities, shyness, and cultural rules may make eye contact uncomfortable. Direct eye contact may be interpreted as challenging authority in some cultures that value deference to leaders. A shy person may feel threatened when an adult makes eye contact too soon. Someone on the autism spectrum, even at the high-functioning end (see chapter 6), is not likely to make eye contact regularly or in a typical way, even after a relationship is established. Bright, sensitive kids may not feel comfortable making eye contact until later in a relationship, because sometimes eye contact is too much stimulation, too distracting from the conversation. They also may experience verbal or nonverbal judgment and shame. We believe that shaming and judgment are not conducive to positive change in counseling—and in general.

Applying the guidelines in this chapter, regardless of circumstances, can help adults develop a trusting relationship with a child or teen, who may never have experienced such a relationship. That relationship might lead to multilevel positive changes in morale, mental health, and behavior.

Not Demanding Information

Even when they have had extensive parenting and/or professional experience with kids, adults should not presume to "know everything about them." When the suggestions and guidelines in this chapter are applied thoughtfully, kids are usually willing to talk about themselves after trust is established—at least a little. But it is not wise to demand personal information. Demands can inhibit comfortable interaction and an optimal therapeutic, parent-child, or teacher-student relationship.

Respecting and Validating

Just a simple, mumbled response can affirm and validate what kids have said. Even a one-syllable response, like the first two points below, can be adequate—and helpful:

- "Wow."
- "Ooooh."
- "That makes sense."
- "Sorry to hear that."
- "Sounds scary/frustrating/upsetting/shocking/overwhelming/difficult."

If the goal is to learn about the internal world of kids, adults should listen carefully and accept that what children and teens say is important from *their* perspective. If the relationship is new, adults might wonder if they are being taken for a ride with animated false or exaggerated details. Even then, however, they can respond, "Wow. That's almost unbelievable. I'll have to think more about that." At another meeting, without smirking, the adult might say, "So that's really what happened? Wow. What did you do then?" If incredible details continue, the adult might ask, "How does it feel when you talk about incredible things like that? If you tell your friends things like that, how do they react?" Of course, some kids' lives are indeed incredible. Respect is key to all relationships, especially with kids. Early, unfounded accusations of lying are not only shaming, but also disrespectful. Continually expressing doubt without evidence of fabrication might ruin prospects for a trusting, life-altering relationship. If lying is indeed occurring, it might actually stop spontaneously when trust has been established and lying no longer has a function (for example, wanting to be interesting, not wanting to talk about serious concerns, believing that truth is dangerous, or having anxiety about talking with an adult).

Keeping the Focus on Kids

When kids describe experiences that remind adults of their own childhood or adolescence, the adults may be tempted to talk about themselves. But they should avoid making the conversation about themselves. Recalling a similar experience is not always inappropriate. Sometimes—though rarely, in our opinion—a brief personal recollection might help to make a point. Dan has found this to be especially effective when working with a bright client who is feeling isolated, different, and not accepted. However, as Jean emphasized when training counselors, it is often difficult to bring the focus fully back to the child or teen after an adult's personal experiences enter the conversation. In her clinical work, she almost never referred to her early life or her family, instead keeping the focus on the student or client, who typically responded with pertinent information and expressive language. Her reasoning for this emphasis in training is that a helping relationship is not about the listener. In addition, kids may only rarely have someone's undivided attention, and even *similar* experiences are not the *same*.

> To learn about kids, adults need to be taught *by* them.

Further, if adults think they can relate to a child or teen only if they have had similar experiences, they are forgetting the many real-life examples that disprove this theory. Other-gender doctors, therapists, and coaches; young caretakers of elderly persons; and substance-abuse clinicians who are not in recovery, for instance, can apply knowledge and skills effectively without having had personal experience with a particular challenge.

Being "Positively Uninformed"

Adults should not assume they know everything they need to know about kids, including bright and extremely talented kids who are also sensitive, discouraged, shy, or unmotivated to achieve in school. Invested adults should also remember that they are not expected to be an expert on child or adolescent development. It's okay to be clueless. To learn about kids, adults need to be taught *by* them. Having listening skills helps them interact confidently during this process.

We underscore here that in order to learn about the internal world of a bright, sensitive child or teen, adults can ask open-ended questions like this one: "What is it like to be twelve in this complicated world?" It's important to remember that a child's experiences are unique to that child. An adult's own childhood doesn't confer knowledge about a child's current life. Even a relatively small difference of five to ten years in age makes an older teen's life experiences different from a young teacher's.

Teachers and school counselors are trained to focus on the student. Even when the adults are middle-aged or near retirement, special skills can help them learn about and appreciate the uniqueness of a child or teen. As educators and parents age, they can still apply listening and responding skills respectfully and compassionately. A learner posture is an essential element.

Self-Regulating

Adults are often involved in guiding children or teens toward better self-regulation, behavior management, and emotional expression. Adults who work with kids likewise need to regulate their own behavior and emotional expression.

- Adults need to refrain from finishing kids' sentences or rescuing them from unsettling emotions or thoughts. Kids need to feel. They need to talk.

- Adults need to stay poised and not overreact, no matter what they hear. If an adult catastrophizes when a child tells them about something terrible, the child perceives that the experience is too much for anyone to hear. Adult poise, with compassionate nonverbal behaviors, says that expressing feelings is okay and that anything can be talked about. Talking with a trustworthy adult can be helpful in itself, regardless of the topic.

- Adults need to self-monitor, be unafraid of feelings, and not be upset by tears. They might say, simply, "It's okay to cry." They can keep a box of tissues handy.

- Adults need to remember that struggle is not a bad thing. In fact, people develop resilience through struggle.

Not Needing to "Fix" Them

Probably most adults can recall the frustration they felt when a friend, spouse, or partner didn't understand that they simply needed to vent about a situation at work or at home or elsewhere. They did not want to be fixed—just heard. They weren't looking for advice. Teachers, parents, and other adults often believe they need to be able to fix problems that kids bring to them. When Jean was training mental health and school counselors, she usually began by saying that her goal was to remove the burden of fixing from their shoulders. Adults need not feel responsible for fixing situations, behaviors, or limitations. In fact, advising, fixing, and rescuing are examples of adult behaviors that can actually *dis*empower kids, who thereafter may need to rely on an adult each time they need to solve a problem.

Instead, even the role of "helping professionals" is to artfully and skillfully help people figure out how to live more effectively—stop negative behavior, develop new and more effective behaviors, resolve interpersonal issues, and feel better, for example. Those who are helped can accomplish goals by applying personal strengths, which usually are illuminated when interacting in individual or group counseling sessions.

What to Avoid

The following are guidelines about what to avoid when listening to children and teens, including those who have high ability:

- Tell yourself to "bite your tongue" if you're tempted to criticize, judge, shame, blame, give advice, preach, or bombard kids with questions. These responses can be barriers to developing a trusting relationship, which is usually key to helping.

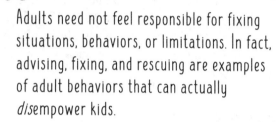

Adults need not feel responsible for fixing situations, behaviors, or limitations. In fact, advising, fixing, and rescuing are examples of adult behaviors that can actually *dis*empower kids.

- Avoid acting bored. If you feel bored, listen harder, make better-quality statements, or ask better open-ended questions—out of respect. No children or teens should sense that an adult listener finds them uninteresting.

- Avoid saying the words *should* and *shouldn't*. This constraint usually helps keep the focus on strengths, assets, and positive behaviors.

- Avoid saying "Yes, but . . ." Those two words invalidate what the child just said. Instead, rein in any impulse to say something judgmental. More helpful might be "You made an interesting choice there." There's value in allowing a child or teen to explore options through talking, without saying "Yes, but wouldn't it have been better if you'd . . . "

- Avoid asking why. Kids usually don't know why they did something or feel a certain way. Knowing why is not as helpful as feeling heard.

- Avoid saying "I know exactly what you mean." Adults really don't know *exactly* what kids mean. Other potentially unhelpful comments are "That happened to me once" and "You have no reason to feel like that."

When you don't understand a response or a particular struggle, ask for help:

- "Help me understand what you meant by . . ."

- "Help me understand what being shy (or having a bad temper, or getting into trouble) is like for you."

Being Patient

Being comfortable with silence is important when talking with anyone, of any age, but especially kids. Giving them time to respond respects that they might want time to think and to consider what they should say. They might need to identify a feeling, gather courage to say something, and decide which words are best to describe something before they speak. A patient listener, comfortable with quietness, may help a child or teen navigate or survive a high-stress situation that is difficult to talk about.

Thanking Kids

It is appropriate for adults to thank kids for talking with them and for helping them understand better what it's like to be their age and live their life. Kids appreciate being commended for their courage and ability to express themselves. Adults should never take for granted that bright, sensitive kids will talk about complex (or even simple) personal matters willingly or eagerly.

ETHICS

The training of clinical professionals includes extensive attention to detailed ethical codes, which will guide their behavior. Teachers, parents, and others who apply the concepts and listening skills in this chapter in schools or other settings also need to be mindful of, for example, personal biases (see chapter 9), the fragility of trust, the importance of respecting and protecting the privacy of kids and their families, and potential voyeurism (that is, meeting their own needs through being enthralled with personal information about kids and families). These aspects are all essential to listening responsibly. We describe two additional ethical concerns next.

False Claims About Training

Adults should not assume the role of psychologist, counselor, or therapist or use one of those words to describe themselves unless they have appropriate credentials. If they claim any of those titles, they are assuming liability. They should have an appropriate degree in hand, training to do what they are doing, and professional liability insurance. School counselors typically have coverage as an employee, but usually also have their own insurance as well, since if a counselor (and, simultaneously, the school district) is accused of malpractice, the district will protect itself first. Unfortunately, the word *counseling* is too often used casually to describe various kinds of advice-giving and consultation. In schools, not only because of constraints on students' autonomy and vulnerability to manipulation, but also because knowledge about career development, resources, and options is important when bright students consider the future, the term *counselor* should be reserved for school and community mental health counselors.

"Playing Psychologist"

Adults should not claim to know what *causes* a problem, or be preoccupied with causes, since communication and life are much more complicated than simplistic causes and effects. Too often, untrained helpers assume that their role is to figure out why a problem is occurring and to offer advice. Those assumptions may prevent careful listening and may reflect a belief that talking, exploring emotions and behaviors, and being heard are not in themselves therapeutically valuable.

We recommend that adults avoid psychoanalyzing even if they do have proper credentials. Analysis and interpretation are usually not helpful in the kinds of conversations we promote in this chapter. Expressing feelings and thoughts can help kids accomplish two worthy goals: gaining insights and making sense of themselves. Talking and listening with anyone individually can be quite therapeutic—even more so in a small group of age peers, and especially when all are similar in ability level. Regardless of ability, however, age peers are likely to find common ground in discussions about social and emotional development. Small-group discussion is discussed further in chapters 8 and 9.

POINTS TO PONDER

- Basic listening and responding skills can help adults learn from bright kids—about how they experience developmental challenges and about how they experience an active brain.

- Even highly invested adults may know little about the internal world of bright kids.

- Assuming a one-down posture (letting kids do the informing) helps adults learn about bright kids' internal world.

- Bright kids benefit when adults not only respect their intellect, talent, and skill, but also pay attention to the social and emotional aspects of growing up.

- Adults who show interest in what having high ability feels like and how it affects life validate the complexity that bright kids live with.

Achieving and Underachieving

SIBLINGS Charlie and Tess, one year apart in age and emotionally close, routinely have 99th-percentile scores on standardized group-administered tests across all areas of the curriculum, and their academic work and behavior are impressive. Throughout elementary and middle school, their teachers smile readily at them and enjoy their delightful humor. Their mother attends parent conferences and hears positive reports.

By mid-autumn in ninth grade, however, Tess has changed. She is often absent, late to class, and late with homework. Her sad, averted eyes suggest disengagement. Her teachers are not aware of her stellar history and are not acquainted with her parents. Charlie, in tenth grade, continues to do well academically, but has already served three Saturday detentions for fighting.

One of each kid's several teachers contacts the school counselor. The counselor checks student records and discovers Tess and Charlie's high ability. However, neither teen is willing to talk with the counselor, and calls to the home are not returned.

Several months later, the local newspaper reports that their father has been arrested for sexual abuse. Teachers and principals connect his last name to Tess and Charlie and begin to make sense of the changes in these bright siblings. Tess is now an academic underachiever. Charlie continues to perform well academically, maintaining control over that part of his life, but he feels intense pain for his sister and deep anger toward his father. The mental health of both teens is precarious.

. . . .

At gifted-education conferences, in textbooks, and in conversations among teachers, stereotypes of gifted high achievers and gifted low achievers abound. Adults often view the former as conscientious, eager, compliant, respectful, socioeconomically advantaged students who do not struggle academically. For most educators and the general public, these students epitomize giftedness. Until high school, Tess and Charlie fit the stereotype of bright kids performing well in the classroom. Those stereotypes don't often allow room for dramatic change in students' lives.

In contrast, adults often view high-ability underachievers—especially teens—as resisting authority and willfully disregarding others' expectations. They're seen as lazy, uninterested in learning, and cynical about school. The default perception is that they could, but *won't,* perform. Tess might have been perceived accordingly, but she didn't "act out"—even with cynical comments. She represents underachievers who *can't* perform, who are overwhelmed by circumstances at a particular time during the school years.

Both of these stereotypes are unfair, inappropriately narrow, and potentially dangerous. Stereotypes of high achievers leave no room for self-doubt, unsettling personal experiences, and stress from their own and others' expectations. When adults hold these stereotypes, they're shocked when high achievers drop out of college, experience mental illness, or die by suicide. Similarly, adults may be astonished when bright teens who dramatically underachieved in high school do well in college. But none of these outcomes is actually rare, as the research described in this chapter will attest.

Each student is much more than what they do—or don't do—academically.

Both bright high achievers and bright underachievers may struggle with developmental tasks: developing identity, establishing direction, experiencing increasingly mature relationships, moving toward autonomy, and gaining a sense of competence. Jean encourages mixing high- and low-achieving gifted kids in small-group discussion, not just because they have the same developmental tasks, but also because these students are likely to be at a similar intellectual level and can learn from each other about relationships, coping with stress, and making decisions. In a mixed group, their specific intellectual strengths and limitations might differ, but an unmixed group of bright students might differ just as much. Acknowledging that both achievers and underachievers experience the asset-burden paradox of giftedness may lead to meaningful conversation that helps them feel connected to their peers. Each student is much more than what they do—or don't do—academically.

In this chapter we present gifted kids at both ends of the *achievement* continuum as being complicated and continually developing. We try to make sense of surprising outcomes. High achievers might not always continue to achieve academically after high school, and underachievers can indeed become achievers. According to Jean's several studies of high and low achievers, which are discussed in chapter 5, both may become surprisingly different in college and beyond. Positive change for underachievers might take the form of improved academic achievement or accomplishing crucial developmental tasks and getting "unstuck," for example. For high achievers it might be an autonomous decision about college major, location, and career path. For both high and low achievers it might be resolving conflict with parents or developing a comfortable identity that incorporates their high ability.

Both high and low achievers may struggle and feel stuck sometimes. Both can benefit from counseling during those times—and from patience in adults who care about them.

This feeling of stuckness may affect many aspects of life, including physical and mental health and motivation to achieve academically.

How adults interact with high and low achievers during the school years matters, especially during the times of little movement ahead. Adults should try not to hang onto the notion that high achievers are "okay" and underachievers are "not okay," and they should try not to think that high academic achievement is the ultimate and most worthy goal during the school years. Ideally, adults see *whole children and teens* when they interact with bright, sensitive individuals—not just stereotypical performers and underperformers.

HIGH ACHIEVERS

Invested adults, including clinical professionals, may not consider that high-performing students can be at risk for poor outcomes. After all, achievers probably appear to manage well socially and academically. Betsy McCoach and Del Siegle (2003) found that achievers distinguish themselves with self-regulation, motivation to achieve, goals, positive self-perceptions about academic ability, and positive attitudes about teachers. Thomas Hébert (2000) found that their parents are likely to be supportive and involved at school, that teachers validate their efforts, and that the achievers themselves are invested in academics and talent areas.

Achievers' work orientation in a talent area, commitment, and enjoyment in doing what they do well are all correlated with *flow*—when a student experiences a balance of challenge and skill and feels engaged to the extent that they are unaware even of time and context (Csikszentmihalyi 1997). High achievers usually have a good fit with classroom expectations. They typically are also the "gifted students" whom researchers study, because being already identified as gifted makes them reasonably accessible. High achievers are far more likely than low achievers to be identified. Identifiers may not question the notion that giftedness means high performance and that only high achievers deserve the attention of special services—though they *should* question it.

However, adults may not have a holistic view of high achievers. A rigorous, accelerated curriculum may not incorporate social and emotional learning or reflect that policy makers and program directors are interested in bright kids' social and emotional development. As a result, high achievers may not consider approaching teachers, counselors, or parents about distress—even extreme distress—related to issues such as bullying (Peterson and Ray 2006), severe family conflict (Peterson 2002), sexual trauma (Peterson 2001a, 2014), depression (Desmet, Pereira, and Peterson 2020; Jackson and Peterson 2003), low sense of direction (Peterson 2001b) and sexual orientation or sexual identity (Peterson 2001a; Peterson and Rischar 2000), for example.

Indeed, high achievers may struggle with depression and have thoughts of suicide. Most will make it through the growing-up years intact, but the school years might be lonely and unsettling—even for those who are well liked and popular and who excel academically and in activities. Because of these students' good record, even school counselors might not think to ask open-ended questions about worries or stress during a perfunctory meeting about a class schedule, a letter of recommendation, or college plans.

When high achievers do seek out a school counselor for support, they probably are relieved when the counselor is *not in awe* of their stellar academic work and talent and is instead focused on their well-being. When there is no need to guard the achiever image, trust and openness can occur in the therapeutic relationship. School counselors can have great impact on the current and future life of high achievers, not least because perfor-mance is not their main or only focus. School counselors and school psychol-ogists are two school professionals who are essentially developmental specialists, aware of what is normal and what is not.

> When there is no need to guard the achiever image, trust and openness can occur.

As high achievers move into young adulthood, community and university counselors and psychologists may see them clinically more than school counselors did. The positive high school image of success gradually fades in importance, and maturity allows them to seek support. Some high achievers are sad and adrift in college, after leaving supportive parents, teachers, and coaches and a strong, positive identity behind.

Development

In our clinical work, we have seen that high achievers can feel high stress because of their own and others' expectations. But they face other social and emotional challenges as well. They may struggle with developmental tasks yet lack opportunities to talk about development.

High achievers may decide prematurely on career direction because of family pressure or because of their own low tolerance for ambiguity, without considering whether that career choice fits well with their personality, interests, needs, and values. They may say, "I just want to have the decision made!" With multiple career paths possible because of their intellectual strengths and talents, they also might dread the thought of leaving viable options behind. High achievers may have a narrow identity, without much sense of self beyond academic performance, being "best," and winning. For some, extended education can delay autonomy, another developmental task, because they remain financially depen-dent on family and are unable to assume responsibility for even small areas of their life, such as food, laundry, or transportation. They may also delay moving toward a mature, potentially long-term relationship with someone special. None of these challenges is inherently negative, but they may differ from the struggles many underachievers have with developmental tasks.

When Jean studied fourteen gifted students (in the top 5 percent on a national measure) who were at risk for poor educational, developmental, and personal (for example, estrangement from family, drug use, disordered eating, sexually transmitted diseases, self-harm, mental health concerns) outcomes after they graduated from high school, two National Merit Scholars were among them (Peterson 2002). Risk factors for all participants were depression and thoughts of suicide, severe family conflict or another extremely challenging family situation, or severe underachievement. Each of the National Merit Scholars returned home for at least a year during college, struggling to find direction. Both eventually found meaningful and atypical employment in music, their main area of interest.

Academic Struggles

Somewhat surprisingly, in two other studies involving high achievers, academic struggles were a major theme. In the study of negative life events during the school years mentioned earlier, the unrelenting stress of advanced academics, school transitions, peer relationships, overcommitment to activities, family situations, and pressure from high expectations were commonly noted as "the most difficult challenges"—not the life events their parents had checked on an annual survey, such as deaths, illnesses, accidents, and relocations (Peterson, Duncan, and Canady 2009).

Jean conducted a study of high academic achievers (68 percent of participants) and low academic achievers (32 percent of participants) four years after high school. In this study, developmental tasks were themes in the participants' language about "biggest challenges": autonomy for 61 percent of participants, social concerns for 27 percent, a significant relationship for 24 percent, adjusting to a new environment for 24 percent, identity for 21 percent, adjusting after an unsettling life event for 21 percent, and career direction for 19 percent. Surprisingly, 51 percent mentioned academic concerns. Regarding career, 42 percent had clear direction after four years, but 30 percent were "not sure at all" (Peterson 2000a).

In other studies, some high achievers became underachievers in late elementary or middle school (Peterson and Colangelo 1996; Peterson 2001a, 2002). At that point, teachers and counselors may not be aware of these students' high intelligence because it has been masked by negative behavior, apathy, or depression. However, in general, high achievers trust the school environment and believe they can succeed in it, believe school is meaningful, are positive about teachers, and therefore engage in school (McCoach and Siegle 2003).

Gifted underachievers trust school less and find less meaning and value in it. Their academic performance differs as a result.

HIGH-ABILITY UNDERACHIEVERS

Underachievement usually means a discrepancy between expected academic achievement (based on some measure of ability) and actual achievement. Jean first became intrigued with the complexity and widely varying personalities of underachievers during twenty years of teaching English and writing and fifteen concurrent years of directing a summer foreign language day camp for early adolescents. In the classroom, those who underachieved in other classes were sometimes the most talented, insightful, and nimble writers. At the camp, those whose parents mentioned underachievement during informal preliminary communication learned as quickly as those identified as high achievers and appeared to have less anxiety. They responded eagerly to the multimodal curriculum and teaching.

When Jean was later invited to lead a gifted-education program in a large high school, she knew she wanted underachievers to be involved in it. She was concerned about the increasing divide between low and high achievers that occurs when advanced courses coincide with adolescence. Half of the twenty-five program options she created were intended to appeal to both high- and low-achieving high-ability kids. (See chapter 5 for more detail.)

However, she learned then, and later as a researcher, that underachievers are difficult to find. She located them, but only with considerable effort. That challenge might be one reason few scholars have studied them. Clinical professionals and teachers both interact with bright underachievers, but teachers may not recognize intellectual strengths if classroom performance is considered the only evidence of intelligence. Even when researchers ask teachers and school counselors to refer students for studies of gifted underachievers, those educators might not view high-ability underachievers as eligible if they believe *gifted underachiever* is an oxymoron—and if they haven't carefully examined the data typically found in individual students' records, such as scores on standardized assessments, widely varying classroom performance across all school years, attendance and lateness, disciplinary referrals, and sometimes teachers' comments from early school years.

GIFTEDNESS RESEARCH CHALLENGES

Because their intellectual strengths are often difficult to identify, underachievers are usually not in samples convenient to access (special programs, advanced classes, or summer enrichment programs) for studies of gifted students. Therefore, research findings related to giftedness usually do not represent a wide range of achievement levels. For example, findings about the mental health status of bright kids may be inappropriately skewed in a positive direction if based mostly on assumptions about achievers or on studies of only achievers, especially if survey and questionnaire items were not informed by complex studies exploring hidden stressors.

The notion that high achievement is necessary for the *gifted* label and for advanced classes is still pervasive. Advanced classes are often the only curriculum in special programs. The potential for a poor fit in advanced classes for students struggling with complicated home or developmental challenges may stop teachers from referring them for further assessment when asked to refer students who might have been missed during screening. Screening is too often limited to scores on group-administered standardized tests. Classroom teachers have considerable power at that juncture. They may not consider that environmental circumstances may affect a bright child's ability to focus on academic work.

In addition, not all high-ability students are highly verbal, contrary to the common assumption—based on potentially skewed samples—that vocabulary is the most reliable indicator of giftedness. Verbal strengths are indeed an asset in most academic areas. But learning disabilities that affect reading and writing can mask intellectual strengths (see chapter 6). In addition, the verbal *assertiveness* often believed to be a "gifted behavior" may be missing (Peterson 2000b).

Underachievers usually do not wave their hands to announce their high ability. Peers and teachers might know that these students are smart, but the term *gifted* probably does not come to mind because of uninspired classroom performance or unwillingness to show what they know on standardized assessments. A cultural emphasis on humility or attentive deference to authority in the classroom might therefore also play a role in the underidentification of gifted underachievers (Peterson 1999).

Having one main teacher during the early school years potentially helps children feel known and nurtured and helps teachers stay alert to individual needs, including when classroom performance declines. Having multiple teachers daily during middle and high school is a major change for students, and the altered morale and lower performance of some might reflect that change. During required check-in meetings during the school year, counselors might not be aware of great discrepancies between measured ability and classroom performance. If aware, these and other adults can ask, "What's different for you this year? What has changed in your life? How is your life going?" Such language is different from the strident language underachievers often hear otherwise: "You could do so much better if you'd just try." Adults need to avoid ineffective and unhelpful blaming, shaming, or "fixing" language, interactions, and attitudes. Instead, they can focus on building and maintaining a trusting relationship and on applying nonjudgmental listening skills (see chapter 3). Bright kids, like those in the general population, may be more likely to thrive when they know they matter—even to just one adult.

> Meeting underachievers where they are, not where adults think they ought to be, is crucial to a supportive relationship with them—and probably to their comfort at school.

Meeting underachievers where they are, not where adults think they ought to be, is crucial to a supportive relationship with them—and probably to their comfort at school. This respectful posture is appropriate no matter how frustrated, pessimistic about a student's future, or concerned about a student's well-being an invested adult is. A relationship with a caring, supportive adult might be central to an underachiever's well-being. Keeping developmental tasks in mind can help adults be compassionate during short- or long-term difficulties at home or at school. Embracing underachievers' complexity is important (for example, "You're an interesting, complicated person, and I appreciate that in you"). Taking advantage of opportunities to interact formally or informally *about development*, referring to "tasks" and "feeling stuck" (see chapters 1, 2, and 5), can also be helpful.

Development

During both childhood and adolescence, bright underachievers may struggle with the same developmental tasks that high achievers struggle with, but the struggles and their effects may look different during the early and later school years. The following examples are intended to provoke thought about those underachievers.

- **Problems with relationships:**
  - » *children* having no mind-mates at school or in the family at their ability level and sharing their interests, or being harassed by peers for being different, with obvious discomfort exacerbating those problems
  - » teachers not encouraging low-performing *teens* to attend college; parents' conditional emotional support or protective hovering inhibiting autonomy development

- **Lack of direction:**
  - » *children* being unable to imagine a future for themselves because strengths are not recognized or because of little or no help with even rudimentary career awareness
  - » *teens* having no available curriculum for career exploration, contributing to low motivation for academic work; low performance masking high ability, affecting interactions with adults

- **Not having a clear sense of self:**
  - » *children* not having classroom opportunities to demonstrate creativity and unusual skills, precluding positive feedback about themselves from teachers and family
  - » *teens* not feeling confident about moving ahead with relationships, career direction, and autonomy

- **An early "mature," sexually active relationship:**
  - » *children* observing negative adult models and listening to their conversations about sexuality, sexual behavior, and relationships
  - » poor modeling leading to high-risk sexual behavior in nonegalitarian relationships as early *teens*, before developing a sense of self, and perceiving that these relationships are "mature"; in contrast, viewing schoolwork as childish

- **Inappropriate, premature autonomy:**
  - » *children* having a parental role in the family instead of being able to rely on a stable, reliable adult for leadership, resulting in a loss of nurturing, loss of childhood
  - » *teens* continuing in this role with anxiety, because they are "the smartest, most responsible one" and their decision-making for the family has become increasingly complex and crucial

- **Problems differentiating emotionally from family:**
  - » *children* witnessing and experiencing poor personal boundaries at home, feeling pulled into ongoing conflicts
  - » *teens* focusing on leaving, bound to parents through conflict, still tied emotionally even from a great distance and self-medicating anxiety and depression with alcohol and other drugs

The developmental stuckness underachievers are likely experiencing may be more obvious than it is with high achievers because of low energy, a dramatic academic downturn, or troublesome behavior. When adults' attention stays focused on behavior, they may miss the anxiety and depression. Unfortunately, at a time when a relationship with a stable, concerned, respectful adult is particularly important, such as during adolescence, some bright, sensitive kids do not have that kind of relationship. Instead, they rely on peers for guidance (Nice 2006).

Bright underachievers may also turn away from academics during a difficult period of development. When they are not identified as having high ability, or when they are accurately identified without appropriate programming available, their well-being can be at risk. When underachievers "fail" in inappropriately narrow programs limited to more-and-faster academics, they may miss official affirmation of abilities, appropriate school support, and opportunity to interact with bright peers.

The developmental tasks listed in the earlier bulleted points are interrelated in many ways. For example, based on our clinical experiences, some bright underachievers may actually explore identity more actively than high achievers do, focusing intensely on peer relationships and boldly changing appearance, interests, and behavior during that exploration. Researchers have challenged the notion that underachievers have a poor academic self-concept, instead calling attention to a low sense of direction and competence and not having goals. Perhaps most important here is that scholars and clinicians have observed that change can happen—as circumstances change and developmental tasks are accomplished. Several of Jean's studies suggest that such a developmental view of underachievement is appropriate, as discussed in chapter 5.

POINTS TO PONDER

- Not all students with high ability are high achievers academically.

- Life events and developmental hurdles can interfere with academic performance.

- High-ability underachievers are often as bright as high achievers—sometimes brighter.

- Expectations from adults and from the kids themselves can add layers of stress for both.

- Preoccupation with performance may mean that the whole child gets little or no attention.

- High-ability children and teens are not merely performers or nonperformers; they are complex humans.

- When invested adults do not see beyond high achievement, they may miss signs of distress.

- Controllable high achievement may mask struggles outside their control.

- Bright high achievers and bright underachievers can learn from each other, including about social and emotional development.

Staying Optimistic About Underachievement

LUIS, D'Andre, Nakry, and Caitlin find common ground in fifth grade when their teachers invite them to form an independent learning team. They meet daily in a school conference room during the teachers' collaboration period. The teachers take turns teaching and planning with them, but the kids work mostly without supervision. Their school records show scores on group ability assessments at or above the 97th percentile in all core areas. (The next-highest scores among classmates are at the 85th percentile.)

Each of the four team members lives with a single parent in an apartment downtown. They live within a few blocks of one another, and their parents use public transportation for work elsewhere in the city. When the parents learn about the independent learning team, they are ecstatic, because their children have been frustrated with the slow classroom pace and have declined in performance. In addition, all four kids developed noticeable attitude and behavior problems over the past four years after parental divorce or death.

The teammates soon plan a weekly after-school club, meeting at Nakry's apartment (the largest available space) to create rules, discuss projects, play games, learn to play an idle guitar, eat (they take turns bringing a snack), and chat. All the kids call their parents at work when they arrive, and Nakry's mother calls home thirty minutes later to check in. A retired teacher lives next door to Nakry and agrees to check on the kids now and then. The kids don't leave until their parents arrive. The parents are all firm about the need to be grateful and trustworthy, respecting belongings in Nakry's home, not taking safety risks, and thanking Nakry's mother and the retired neighbor. In the summer after fifth grade, the kids stay in touch.

The arrangement works well until middle school begins in sixth grade and the team's support structure dissolves. Interests take the kids in new directions, new social groups emerge, and adolescent developmental struggles preoccupy them. The grades and behavior of two of the kids decline but rebound in ninth grade because an alert teacher reminds them that colleges look at performance from that year forward. The other two kids find new mind-mates and continue to do well.

> Underachievement is mostly developmental. When invested adults have a whole-child view, they can purposefully avoid judgmental language and have a positive, supportive relationship instead.

When parents seek counseling for a bright child or teen, academic underachievement is often a concern. Teachers may have given up on an unengaged underachiever, conscious of the needs of others in the class, and parents may be losing patience after seeing no improvement. Finding an effective strategy for resolving academic underachievement quickly is unlikely, and fixing may not be an appropriate short-term goal. Complex, interconnected aspects make poor classroom performance by bright, complicated kids difficult to address, especially with the overlay of developmental, school, or home stressors. However, educators can help low achievers survive the school years and thrive afterward by developing relationships with them and creating programs and activities in which underachievers interact with intellectual peers and remain engaged at school.

Jean's studies of high-ability underachievers, presented later in this chapter, give reasons for hope. She has concluded that underachievement is mostly developmental. When invested adults have a whole-child view, they can purposefully avoid judgmental language and have a positive, supportive relationship instead. They can also remind themselves to be patient. Change in underachievement, just like onset, is not likely to happen quickly.

Professionals in the field of gifted education do a lot of measuring. Through surveys, questionnaires, and quantifiable responses to oral assessments, they measure intelligence, classroom and standardized-test performance, percent of various racial and ethnic groups in gifted-education programs, prevalence of bullying among high-ability kids, and more. After measuring the discrepancy between ability and performance to identify underachievers for research, measurers may then try to determine what causes underachievement and how to reverse it. However, broad findings about causes (such as lack of motivation, goals, self-regulation, and engagement) may not be helpful for individual underachievers, their families, community therapists, and counselors. In fact, we intentionally avoid "cause" language in this book. Instead, we focus on how adults can help underachievers make sense of how they feel, think, and behave. Bright kids want to make sense of themselves. It's therefore important to appeal to their cognitive strengths, including when exploring social and emotional development.

Change—positive and negative—is the focus of this chapter. As clinical professionals, we view underachievers as being much more complicated than simply "unmotivated," "lazy," "rebellious," "sullen," "disengaged," or "too social." Jean's interest as a researcher was in their social, emotional, developmental, and systems-based (school and family) concerns, aspects important for well-being and success in school. Because these are not easily measured, she used qualitative methods (interviews, letters, or open-ended questionnaires) to explore underachievement. Sensitive, complicated underachievers talked or wrote about how they experienced it.

LEARNING GRADUALLY ABOUT BRIGHT KIDS

When Jean taught literature and writing to adolescents, she noticed that the excellent writers and thinkers who were not performing well elsewhere varied greatly in mental health, family circumstances, socioeconomic status, social skills, personality, behavior, involvement in activities, and personal strengths and limitations. She also observed that achievement level did not always predict future success. Some high achievers were not able to complete the first year at a university (because of homesickness, depression, poor fit with institution, or poor fit with urban or rural context, for example), and some high school underachievers fared well. These variances intrigued her, and she became interested in the social and emotional development of both high and low achievers with high ability.

Later, when she was asked to create a gifted-education program in a large high school, she knew she wanted underachievers involved. She believed they should have opportunities to interact with intellectual peers, even if they didn't want to, or couldn't, participate in advanced courses *at that time in their development.* Therefore, the program she developed for 140 students included many stimulating weekly options that high and low achievers could enjoy together. Many of the replicable components in the table below were led by community volunteers. Most components had a social, interactive dimension. *Offerings involving both achievers and underachievers are italicized.*

Future Problem Solving Program	*weekly after-school lectures by community volunteers*	*noon-hour philosophy class*
classical music appreciation	*breakfast club for writing and sharing free-verse poetry*	*creative writing after school*
National History Day	college courses—dual enrollment	independent study
mime	*contemporary dance*	small-group independent study
Chinese language	*Arabic language*	Advanced Placement (AP) courses
American Sign Language (ASL)	*Testing out of some nondifferentiated required classes*	local engineering field trips
Spanish, French, German, or ASL teaching in elementary schools—after school	*career shadowing—one full day only, once per student*	*weekly small-group discussion of nonacademic, development-oriented topics*
collaboration with art teacher for competitions, exhibitions		

Within four years, 85 percent of all students who had been identified as gifted at some point in their education, *one-third of them underachievers*, were participating in the voluntary program, mostly for no transcript credit. However, a monthly newsletter acknowledged community volunteers and listed student participants, leading to credit in the form of substantive casual teacher-student conversations initiated by curious teachers.

Nearly one hundred students were involved in weekly discussion groups, the most popular option. Two discussions, each one hour in length, fit into the daily extended lunch period. The Future Problem Solving Program involved twenty-four students on six teams, and twenty students attended the lunch-hour philosophy class. Thirty to eighty students attended the weekly after-school lectures, presented by local professionals from a wide variety of fields and open to the entire student body. Content routinely went beyond the school curriculum. Some teachers gave extra credit for attending lectures pertinent to their classes, and some of those teachers attended as well. Art exhibits, mime, dance, and classical music appreciation were also open to any interested student. This strategy quietly challenged assumptions about gifted-education elitism and did not compromise program rigor. Many students who had missed the cut for program participation attended the lectures and other open options regularly.

The small-group discussions focused on topics such as strengths and limitations, stress, sensitivity, intensity, perfectionism, learning preferences, peer relationships, social aggression and bullying, family roles, dealing with authority, depression, anxiety, feeling stuck, envisioning the future, and matching a career with personality, interests, and needs. High achievers and underachievers were intentionally mixed in each group of eight to ten students, since both had high ability and both were developing socially and emotionally. They quickly moved past stereotype-based assumptions and replaced competition and suspicion with self-reflection and mutual learning. Jean learned about their developmental challenges. The underachievers were often the most articulate contributors. She wondered if that was because of extensive self-reflection about their low achievement, because they had struggled with difficult life circumstances, or because social interaction was their priority. Several said they had been high achievers until fifth or sixth grade.

All participants had been invited into the program because of high scores on standardized ability or achievement tests in one or more areas represented in the program. The discussion groups absorbed the widest range of ability levels and interests. In a noncompetitive, nonjudgmental setting, quite different from high-pressure academic classrooms and talent areas, they learned from each other about growing up. A teacher referred one memorable participant for his remarkable ability in an advanced drafting class. When Jean checked his thick special-services file for supportive data, she found he had hit the ceiling (highest score possible) in nonverbal intelligence on two tests, quite different from his low-average verbal scores. She talked with him about spatial giftedness, invited him to join a group, and he attended faithfully, sitting quietly each week, listening to more verbal group members.

Five years of the small-group discussions led Jean to pursue counseling degrees and development-oriented research focused on bright kids. She was especially interested in how bright, complicated children and teens experience exceptional ability and if and how school and home influence underachievement. Many findings were unexpected. Some of these studies, summarized in the remainder of this chapter, offer reasons for parents, teachers, and clinical professionals to be optimistic about the future for underachievers. *Findings, speculations, and assertions offering hope for underachievers are italicized.*

DEVELOPMENTAL STUDIES OF UNDERACHIEVEMENT
Examining Student Records

In her first research project, Jean looked for patterns in school records of 153 students in seventh through twelfth grade eligible for gifted-education programs in the district where she had most recently taught. Gifted underachievers had been identified, giving her rare access and opportunity to compare them with achievers. At graduation, students were categorized as HA (high achievers with A grades and 90th to 99th percentile class rank); MA (moderate achievers with B grades and 75th to 89th percentile class rank); MU (moderate underachievers with C grades and 50th to 74th percentile class rank); and EU (extreme underachievers with D or F grades and class rank below the 50th percentile). Findings are summarized below.

- **Performance differences:** Uneven performance was not unusual: 54 percent of total participants (including one-third of the achievers) had at least one semester of under-achievement (UA); 14 percent continued to perform well in one subject area during periods of underachievement. In general, underachievers (UAs) took fewer demanding courses than achievers did but *avoided undemanding courses.* Most UA was chronic, lasting nine or more of twelve semesters.

- **Change:** *20 percent of UAs improved before leaving high school.*

- **Attendance:** UAs in general, and female UAs, were absent more than achievers were. UAs were late to school more than achievers were (35 percent of UAs versus 5 percent of achievers).

- **Gender:** More girls than boys had short-term UA (one to four semesters). However, 91 percent of boys and 41 percent of girls who graduated in a UA category were UAs in seventh grade.

- **College readiness:** *The mean percentile rank was similar for achievers and UAs (93.42 versus 86.89)* on the ACT (American College Testing) exam, and 41 percent of UAs, including five EUs, had composite ACT scores at or above the 90th percentile.

- **Development:** UA became established in middle school for many.

Speculation About Development, Based on Patterns

Underachievement may become established in middle school because of challenges related to identity and self-image, social priorities, direction, autonomy, sexuality, and sense of competence. Chronic underachievement may be due to developmental or systemic factors and/or personal characteristics; short-term underachievement may be related to a course, life event, teacher, or skill gap. Problems with attendance and tardiness may represent passive resistance to authority—silently choosing, with inaction and without drama, not to comply with institutional rules.

Achievement habits may help achievers maintain academic success after negative life events; underachievement habits may make regaining momentum difficult. *Achievement may improve late in high school because of advanced and more varied academic options and the resolution of some social and emotional concerns. Underachievers may maintain achievement in one area because of a teacher, interest in that area, or personal fit with that area, helping them stay engaged at school. Choosing demanding courses, even without performing well in them, brings underachievers into contact with intellectual peers and helps them protect a "smart" image and prepare for college.* But absences and taking fewer demanding courses may affect performance on college-readiness tests. *Avoiding undemanding courses can protect relationships, the college option, and public image. UAs' college aptitude test scores, which do not differ greatly from achievers', may make up for low classroom performance when UAs apply for admission.* Especially if underachievers have not lost confidence due to lack of positive teacher and parent feedback, *college-readiness tests are a chance to show what they know.*

Assertion Supported by Findings
Improved achievement is possible during high school.

A Follow-Up Study Four Years Later
Curious about how the achievers and underachievers fared after graduation, and whether teachers who expected a bleak future for underachievers were correct, Jean sent a questionnaire to the same students four years later. Of the original participants, 63 percent responded, with the percent in each achievement category similar to the percent in those categories in the original study. The achievement categories used in the first study were used again.

- **College or university attendance:** *Low achievement did not preclude higher education: 87 percent of UAs attended college, and 52 percent had four years of college. Of EUs, 82 percent attended college, 56 percent had four years, 44 percent had two to three years, and 2 EUs with high ACT scores had four years. Of HAs, 83 percent had four years of college, 47 percent remained HAs, and 30 percent became UAs. Of UAs with ACT scores above the 90th percentile, 70 percent had four college years.*

- **Academic performance:** *Of UAs, 41 percent improved academically in college, and 26 percent became achievers. UA continued for 44 percent, but one of those underachievers had an engineering degree from a reputable university. Of the UAs who improved in high school, 55 percent continued to improve. Of those with at least one semester of HA in high school, 71 percent had higher achievement in college.*

- **Difficult challenges:** Developmental challenges were often themes in responses to an open-ended question about "difficult challenges": autonomy, 61 percent (of all participants); significant relationship, 24 percent; identity, 21 percent; career direction, 19 percent. Other concerns were academic, 51 percent; social, 27 percent; new environment, 24 percent; critical event, 21 percent; financing education, 18 percent. Ten individuals mentioned a major crisis (illness, death in family, accident), and others mentioned parental separation, divorce, remarriage, or their own struggles with sexual orientation.

- **Sureness of career direction:** Of all participants, 30 percent were "not sure at all" about career direction; 42 percent were "very sure." Nine participants (seven achievers, two UAs) had four years of college, but were "not sure at all." *Achievers and underachievers changed majors and colleges at a similar rate.*

- **Life satisfaction:** *Achievers and UAs were similar in level of life satisfaction.*

Speculation About Development, Based on Findings

After years of anger and frustration, overt or silent rebellion, grief over loss, or developmental stuckness, many UAs, even EUs, are ready to engage academically in college. However, social, emotional, and other developmental challenges have impact on the college experience. High achievement does not ensure satisfaction with life or sureness of direction, *but UAs are not less sure or satisfied.*

Assertions Supported by Findings

Bright underachievers can perform well on college-readiness tests, roughly 80 percent attend college, the majority graduate in four years, and one in four becomes an achiever. High college aptitude test scores and some achievement in high school make improved achievement likely in college.

Successful Adults Who Were Adolescent Underachievers

A study of thirty-one successful adults who had underachieved as adolescents focused on onset, maintenance, and reversal of academic underachievement. All participants had been successful academically during their elementary school years, but then performed poorly for several years. *All of them changed in a positive direction after high school, but not until late in college or graduate school* (for two participants, the change occurred at age thirty-five). Themes associated with underachievement in the language of participants were as follows:

- underinvolved, indifferent, and unencouraging parents and teachers

- negative parent attitudes toward work, education, women, women's work

- good behavior masking depression, family problems, silent conflict with a parent

- heavy home responsibilities

- lack of career direction

- difficult family and school transitions

- adults not recognizing a need for encouragement, respect, validation, "push"
- sibling rivalry
- pressure to perform; unwelcome fuss about achievement
- academics a low priority during a painful, distressing adolescence

Themes associated with onset of underachievement were these:

- family problems
- school milieu (teacher attitudes, teaching methods, gender differences in who was given attention, poor fit with school, peers focused on social life)
- transitions (to new location, new school)
- heavy, adult-level home responsibilities

Reversal of underachievement was associated with these themes:

- *mentors or same-gender achieving role models outside of the family*
- *achievement-oriented peers*
- *accomplishing developmental tasks (identity, direction, mature relationship, autonomy)*
- *changes in location (moving away for college, graduate school)*
- *change in available curriculum*
- *acknowledging that childhood had been abnormal*
- *teacher feedback about academic work*
- *high achievement in activities*
- *personality (such as "feisty," argumentative women)*

Speculations About Development, Supported by Findings

Situations associated with onset or reversal offer possible directions for parents and counselors during bright kids' developmental and other transitions and for teacher-parent conversations.

Assertions Supported by Findings

Role models and friends who are achievers, teachers who give feedback, informal mentors, and success in activities can help underachievers stay engaged when they cannot, or lack motivation to, achieve academically. Motivation to continue education may occur after two or more developmental tasks are accomplished—without particular interventions. Leaving home can provide distance from pressure to perform and space to develop a sense of self, career direction, objectivity about school and family, and less emotional reactivity to family interactions.

Bright, High-Risk High School Students: What Happens to Them?

With their parents' permission, Jean followed fourteen gifted-identified students at high risk for poor personal and educational outcomes (because of severe underachievement, depression, or severe conflict with parents) for four years after high school. Based on the categories used in the first two studies in this section, one student was a high achiever; one was a moderate achiever, four were moderate underachievers, and eight were extreme underachievers. Initially they completed assessments about family satisfaction, leadership, and communication. These one-time assessments revealed the following:

- 86 percent reported low satisfaction with family

- 64 percent perceived high family stress

- 79 percent believed their family was "disengaged," lacking cohesion

- 50 percent assessed family adaptability as "chaotic" or "rigid," the unhealthy extremes

Thereafter, they periodically filled out a brief survey about four areas of development and wrote a note or letter elaborating on their self-assessments. Participants were contacted semiannually for two years, then annually.

Several findings inspire hope for troubled underachievers:

- *Three women had graduated from college, including two extreme underachievers who had reported healthy family cohesion.*

- *Five more had at least three years of college.*

- *Four of those and three more had returned to college after life-altering experiences,* such as world travel financed by seasonal work in Alaska, Semester at Sea, fossil digs with professional paleontologists, dancing professionally in Japan, working in a bank.

- *Accomplishing two or more developmental tasks (such as identity, mature relationship, autonomy, direction, resolving conflict with parents) preceded motivation to pursue further education. Of the eight who experienced a convergence of task accomplishments, four reported "new" motivation.*

- *Conflict with parents generated the most writing by the participants. Autonomy was usually the task accomplished first.*

Having multiple career options seemed to make developing direction difficult. Nine of the fourteen had no clear career direction at the end. Nine reported poor mental health during the study—depression, suicidal thoughts, or drug abuse.

Of the two National Merit Scholars involved, one, a high achiever, had accomplished only one developmental task by the end of the study; the other, a moderate underachiever, had accomplished none. Of the fourteen participants, three were still at high risk personally and educationally at the end of the study; the others were on solid ground.

Speculation About Development, Supported by Findings

Family disengagement can affect achievement and decisions about education. *Accomplishing a mature relationship can help resolve conflict with parents.* Geographic distance may, but does not necessarily, result in being less hyperresponsive to family conflict.

Assertions Supported by Findings

Geographical distance from home and meaningful independent experiences are beneficial for some high-risk young adults. Both achievers and underachievers—even National Merit Scholars— can struggle with developmental tasks. *Extreme underachievers may accomplish key developmental tasks after leaving home, including leaving for college.*

Bright, Troubled Underachievers

Because of her interest in how high-ability students who do not fit "gifted" stereotypes experience development, Jean conducted an interview study of eleven middle-school students, ages eleven to thirteen, from low-income families. They were roughly one-third of the students invited to join small discussion groups after school counselors had suspected that the parents abused drugs. Jean led the groups as a community agency counselor, and after realizing that these eleven students were quite bright, she secured permission to examine their school records to confirm her impressions.

Standardized test scores at an earlier age for these students were at or above the 90th percentile; some were above the 98th percentile. None of the students performed well academically. A teacher had recognized the intelligence of the boy with the highest standardized test scores at age eight, but his mother, who had a severe substance-abuse problem, would not give permission for him to participate in the gifted-education program. No one pursued the matter further. In general, though the eleven participants' high ability was generally invisible to peers and teachers, school seemed to be a positive place for them. Several themes emerged in the language of these bright kids, whose parents did not advocate for them and whose intelligence was not validated in school:

- difficult family circumstances
- no perceived acknowledgement or support for their abilities and strengths at school
- pride in being able to "use my mind" in practical problem-solving
- familiarity with danger and violence
- no involvement in school activities (unreliable transportation)
- a dismal view of the future—or no view of it
- adultlike responsibilities at home
- resilience

Speculation About Development, Supported by Findings

Complex family circumstances can make it difficult for educators and school counselors to have impact on the lives of bright children and teens living with adversity. *However, school professionals can engage, encourage, and support students in creative, substantial ways, steering them toward enrichment opportunities or services at school or in the community, validating their intellectual strengths and talents, and helping them develop direction for the future.*

Assertions Supported by Findings

Bright children in adversity develop practical skills, personal strengths, self-sufficiency, and resilience.

Six Exceptional Young Women, Struggling

With a similar purpose and again through in-depth interviews, Jean studied six bright young women who varied in age. In self-presentation, articulateness, and interests, they appeared to be typical female adolescents with high ability. However, their hold on life was tenuous, and their language reflected major struggles: troubling life events, extremely difficult family situations, one or both parents not functioning well, lack of transportation for school activities and feeling disrespected when involved in them, and for some, often being left in charge of the household. One of these young women was a popular class valedictorian, and she believed no teacher suspected that her home environment was so chaotic. Other themes were noise, commotion, and violence at home that interfered with homework; frequent thoughts of suicide or actual suicide attempts; not enough energy available for academics; not telling teachers about difficulties at home; parents' preoccupation with self, limiting their ability to support their children emotionally; and feeling responsible for parents' unhappiness.

According to test data or grades, each of the young women was quite intelligent and had a pleasant personality. Four came from middle- to upper-middle-income homes. *All were academically successful at some point.* However, three were not identified as having high ability, and they finally doubted their abilities when circumstances affected academic achievement. During middle and high school, three underachieved academically, and *three were achieving*, but living dangerously. All experienced depression and suicidal ideation and needed emotional support.

Speculation About Development, Supported by Findings

Adults paying attention to, and solidly supporting, individual children and teens with high-stress home lives may be crucial to their survival. Teachers and counselors facilitating connection with intellectual peers through creative programming can help bright, high-risk girls recognize their personal strengths and resilience and envision a positive future. Their development continues during and after adolescence, sometimes remarkably positively.

Assertions Supported by Findings

Some bright kids live in difficult circumstances and experience chronic distress, but their compliant behavior and positive demeanor can mask this distress and prevent attention to their underachievement. Assumptions about their having private space at home conducive to homework, or a bed that is always theirs, or nutritious food to eat may be erroneous. However, alert teachers can recognize that average grades may underestimate what these students are learning, that *intelligence helps them make sense of their situations and personal strengths*, and that teachers can offer crucial support during crises.

A Study of Negative Life Events

An eleven-year study involved an annual negative-life-event checklist for parents of gifted students (121 families involved at the outset, 63 at the end) and, at graduation, an open-ended questionnaire about "biggest challenges" and "most positive experiences" for 59 of the students. According to the checklist, these teens, who generally fit positive giftedness stereotypes, experienced a high number of unsettling life events during the school years. When 91 families were still involved, students had experienced 94 deaths of someone close, 77 serious illnesses in extended family, 17 major changes in family, 15 new or chronic illnesses in the student, 11 serious student injuries or surgeries, and 10 deaths of a friend. To the checklist, a few parents added one of the following:

- family financial reversal
- student mental illness diagnosis
- incarceration of parent or well-liked teacher
- severe conflict with teacher
- sexual abuse

In order from most to least mentioned, students mentioned these in response to the question about "three biggest challenges": academics; family and school transitions; college decisions; peer relationships; overcommitment or overinvolvement; death of someone close; family difficulties, injury, illness, or accident; heavy expectations; and rejection. In order from most to least mentioned, students listed these as "most positive, satisfying personal experiences": academics, activities, family/peers, service, and profound life changers.

Speculation About Development, Supported by Findings

Because the negative life events in the checklist were not connected to academics, we might assume that bright achievers and bright underachievers experience a similar number of events. Habits of achievement (such as finding a comfortable groove of self-discipline, good results, satisfaction, and positive thoughts associated with success) may help achievers maintain or recover high performance during difficult times. Habits of underachievement (academic work not associated with good results, satisfaction, and positive thoughts) may inhibit rebounding during and after adversity. The narrative responses of achievers and

UAs to open-ended questions about challenges reflected the "habits" language described above. Developmentally, for both high achievers and underachievers, "going beyond" in extracurricular activities or involvement in the broader community can contribute to vision and direction, confidence in competence, social connections, spiritual growth, a sense of fulfillment, and additional opportunities.

Assertions Supported by Findings

Bright kids experience a high number of unsettling events during the school years, with potential impact on achievement. In spite of those challenges, most achieve in the class-room and *find satisfaction in intense, sometimes life-altering, involvement in school and/or community activities.*

Summary of Peterson Studies

The studies described in this chapter suggest that underachievers' lives outside of school vary in many ways, that complicated life circumstances and negative life events are more common among high-ability children and teens than educators realize, and that many contributors to poor academic performance are not easily changed. However, findings also offer hope to underachievers and the adults who care about them. *Many underachievers eventually accomplish developmental tasks and move forward.* However, because struggles with developmental tasks are common, both achievers and underachievers can benefit from proactive attention to social and emotional development throughout the school years. The first four studies, focused on development, revealed that predicting the future on the basis of only one developmental stage is unwise. The last three studies call attention to experiences with potential impact on development and on motivation to achieve academically.

POINTS TO PONDER

- Complicated life circumstances and negative life events are common among bright kids.

- Academic performance may not be a priority for bright kids who are in challenging situations or who are developmentally "stuck."

- Developing a respectful, nonjudgmental relationship with underachievers may be the most important action adults can take.

- Developmental tempo may vary over the school years, depending on circumstances.

- Accomplishing specific developmental tasks may lead to being able to focus on academic work, including long after the K–12 school years.

- Positive change in school performance can happen as life circumstances change.

- Each underachiever interacts uniquely in counseling, in the classroom, and at home.

- Invested adults, armed with the information from this chapter, can avoid strident, ineffective language and speak confidently about the probability of change.

- Bright students in distress may not seek out school counselors—perhaps because those counselors are often stereotyped as being "for other kids, not smart kids," or because they believe they should be able to "figure things out" by themselves.

Living on the Edges, Twice-Exceptionally

LOUKA is ten years old and in fifth grade. He is a deep, abstract thinker and asks endless questions in class, often occupying a lot of his teacher's time. He usually answers all questions on tests correctly, but he seldom turns in homework. He talks incessantly and moves around the classroom constantly. His talking distracts his classmates, and he is seen as a know-it-all.

. . . .

ISABELLA is a highly creative eight-year-old girl who writes elaborate poetry and imaginative stories. She is in third grade, but she reads at an eighth-grade level. She has difficulty transitioning to a new activity or subject in the classroom. She often seems lost in thought. Her teachers can't figure out how to keep her engaged in class and how to help her avoid melting down when changes occur.

. . . .

MARCOS, a thirteen-year-old in seventh grade, is a puzzle to his teachers and parents. He has always had a large vocabulary and elaborate ideas, yet his writing skill is only basic. He refuses to read, saying it is boring. He won't write down his assignments; he says he will remember what he needs to do. He often doesn't finish tests because he runs out of time, but the questions he responds to are complete and correct.

. . . .

Louka, Isabella, and Marcos exemplify twice-exceptionality—being bright with a disability. These children show a pattern of advanced abilities and coexisting characteristics that contributes to learning problems and/or social problems and may be at the root of their lagging behind academically. When we work with twice-exceptional (2e) kids clinically, we often find perplexing conundrums. Their parents may say, "We know they are bright, but . . . ," and then we anticipate the rest: they have sloppy handwriting, they can write only at a basic level, they don't follow directions, they perform poorly on tests, and so on.

> When a child has extreme asynchrony, or highly varied abilities, twice-exceptionality is likely.

In chapter 2, we discussed asynchronous development in bright individuals—advanced abilities coexisting with typical or low-level skills. When a child has extreme asynchrony, or highly varied abilities, twice-exceptionality is likely. Twice-exceptional kids show advanced abilities as well as delayed ability development, and they often have a label or diagnosis explaining their area of challenge. These areas of challenge cause additional burdens and stress, which we discuss in chapter 7.

DEFINITION

The Twice-Exceptional Community of Practice (2e CoP), a diverse group of educators, advocates, and psychologists, including Dan, created this definition of twice-exceptionality and its ramifications:

> Twice-exceptional individuals evidence exceptional ability and disability, which results in a unique set of circumstances. Their exceptional ability may dominate, hiding their disability; their disability may dominate, hiding their exceptional ability; each may mask the other so that neither is recognized or addressed.
>
> 2e students, who may perform below, at, or above grade level, require the following:
>
> - Specialized methods of identification that consider the possible interaction of the exceptionalities
>
> - Enriched/advanced educational opportunities that develop the child's interests, gifts, and talents while also meeting the child's learning needs
>
> - Simultaneous supports that ensure the child's academic success and social-emotional well-being, such as accommodations, therapeutic interventions, and specialized instruction
>
> Working successfully with this unique population requires specialized academic training and ongoing professional development. (Baldwin, Baum, and Hughes 2015)

A critical aspect of understanding 2e individuals is how their behavior may vary from one situation or context to another. At home, a child who knows everything about wormholes and astrophysics may not be able to get dressed independently. Perhaps a child who writes beautiful, expressive poetry about the complexities of life cannot make or keep a friend. A teen who can debate politics and the economy at an impressive level may have extreme temper tantrums like a three-year-old when told to stop playing a video game. These developmental paradoxes can make parenting difficult, a challenge addressed in chapter 12.

IMPACT AT SCHOOL

So how is twice-exceptionality displayed at school? Many scenarios are possible. A 2e child's strengths and weaknesses can cancel out each other. As a result, the child may perform "fine," "average," or "at grade level"—and therefore miss out on needed services. All too often the ramifications of twice-exceptionality, such as the following, go unrecognized or unaddressed:

- fatigue (difficulty focusing on classwork, falling asleep, irritability)
- frustration
- self-criticism ("I'm stupid")
- hopelessness
- underachievement
- anxiety
- depression

Bright, sensitive children and teens often have high expectations for themselves. Falling short of meeting those may take an emotional toll on them and their families. Identifying and understanding the challenges of twice-exceptionality can help 2e kids and their parents make sense of the kids' behaviors.

COMMON 2E DIAGNOSTIC LABELS

Understanding a bright child's challenges helps adults provide support and interventions. Following is a nonexhaustive list of diagnoses commonly associated with twice-exceptionality:

- **autism spectrum disorder (ASD):** What was formerly called Asperger's disorder, separate from ASD, involves difficulty engaging in back-and-forth communication and noticing and understanding social nuances, processing sensory stimulation, and managing unexpected changes, for example. Now, Asperger's is included on the ASD spectrum, but "at the top end" because high intellectual ability is a component. Two or three decades ago, Asperger's was not on counselors', educators', and parents' radar. Now it is, helping diagnosed children and people involved with them make sense of strengths and limitations. Because bright adolescents today may have been diagnosed with Asperger's earlier and may still identify with this diagnosis, we are including it here. With supports and social skill-building at school, children and teens diagnosed with ASD and fitting previous clinical understanding of Asperger's may have success in careers that fit their strengths and are not hindered by their limitations.

- **attention deficit hyperactivity disorder (ADHD):** developmentally inappropriate levels of inattention, hyperactivity, and impulsivity, indicating deficits in executive functioning—the ability to engage in purposeful, organized, strategic, self-regulated, goal-directed behavior

- **dyslexia:** difficulty learning and processing reading and writing, despite adequate intelligence, instruction, and motivation
- **dyscalculia:** difficulty with number sense, facts, and calculation; formulas; spatial relations; and mathematical reasoning
- **dysgraphia:** deficit in fine-motor functioning, which affects writing
- **sensory processing disorder (SPD):** difficulty with various sensory systems and motor systems not working together (for example, difficulty with muscle control or difficulty regulating sensory input, such as light or sound)
- **auditory processing disorder (APD):** trouble processing and making meaning of sounds; challenges related to filtering out what is said when there is background noise
- **visual processing disorder:** challenges with eye tracking, decoding, sustaining focus on symbols (such as words and numbers), and reading letters or numbers, which appear to blur, move, or rotate

Anxiety and depression can be either primary or secondary diagnoses, depending on assessment. Mood disorders such as anxiety, depression, and bipolar disorder, when present without any of the diagnoses listed above, still qualify as exceptionalities and often have great impact on life at and outside of school. Anxiety and depression are concerns that need prompt attention and treatment.

WHAT TO LOOK FOR

We often say that "locating a 2e child is not rocket science," for there are familiar patterns that indicate a need for formal (testing) or informal (classroom performance) assessment to find out what is happening. However, a combination of the No Child Left Behind Act in 2002, the Individuals with Disabilities Education Improvement Act (IDEIA) in 2004, more recent changes in educational law and interpretations of the law, and economic crises have made it difficult to dig deeper. These factors have resulted in a drastic reduction of testing to evaluate students, changes in the interpretation of test results, and some states designating minimum cut scores to qualify for any special education services (Gilman et al. 2013; Gilman and Peters 2018).

In addition, a US regular education initiative called Response to Intervention (RTI) was introduced in 2004 with the reauthorization of the Individuals with Disabilities Education Act (IDEA). RTI calls for teachers to identify students who are performing below grade level and offer evidence-based interventions to address the observed problem. Those who do not respond positively to the intervention receive higher levels of intervention in the regular education setting. This stage of the process means delayed special education evaluations, understanding the child's challenges, and implementing effective interventions (Gilman and Peters 2018). Because most 2e children are able to perform academically at least at low average to average levels due to their advanced cognitive abilities, 2e students are often not identified as having a learning or developmental problem. When a bright child is performing at grade level, meeting minimum grade criteria, and scoring in the average or even above-average range on standardized tests, it is difficult for educators to recognize, understand, and make an argument that a challenge or disability is affecting classroom work.

Only trained professionals can make mental health, behavioral, and developmental diagnoses and diagnose learning disorders. Diagnoses are often made based on interview, observation, and developmental history and evaluation. Commonly, neuropsychologists, clinical psychologists, educational psychologists, and psychiatrists make diagnoses. School psychologists use testing to identify learning and processing issues, but rather than diagnosing, they determine whether a child meets criteria for an individualized education program (IEP) for a specific learning disability, ASD, emotional disturbance, or other conditions which qualify as "other health impaired." Additional licensed professionals who diagnose are family practitioners, pediatricians, developmental and behavioral pediatricians, developmental optometrists, speech and language pathologists, audiologists, and occupational therapists. Parents, guardians, and teachers cannot diagnose, but can notice and report discrepancies associated with twice-exceptionality. Some characteristics of bright kids who struggle with one or more other exceptionalities are these:

- high verbal abilities, but average academic performance
- mismatched performance and perceived potential
- poor handwriting; mixture of uppercase and lowercase letters and words
- poor spelling; can't retain memorized spelling words
- failure to respond to literacy efforts that emphasize *more* reading; reading level improved by the end of the school year, but gains lost by the end of summer
- difficulty memorizing math facts
- frustration with being required to show what they know, in general, and to "show their work" in mathematics
- poor body control; impulsive responding
- trouble understanding social situations and reading other people's nonverbal behaviors

If a child or teen has some of the above-mentioned characteristics and is struggling despite personal effort and teacher support, a closer look through comprehensive assessment is warranted. The "Checklist for Recognizing Twice-Exceptional Children," created by Linda Silverman, Barbara Gilman, Deirdre Lovecky, and Elizabeth Maxwell (2019), can help parents, teachers, and counselors identify 2e individuals' areas of strength and challenge and, if advisable, make recommendations for further assessment and services.

TESTING

Having a bright child tested by a professional trained in using assessments to identify learning disabilities can illuminate issues related to development, learning, or processing (speed of understanding and producing information). Testing can help adults understand a child's learning and processing profile and can guide them when planning curriculum differentiation and accommodation of strengths, limitations, and needs. Comprehensive testing is necessary because cognitive abilities, academic abilities, attention, executive functioning skills, and mood and behavior all need to be assessed. When warranted, social understanding and processing should also be assessed. (See the example of Andrew in chapter 11.) The National Association for Gifted Children (NAGC) recommends that schools "provide comprehensive assessment (including norm-based, psychometrically sound, comprehensive individual intelligence and achievement tests and measures in all areas of observed strength and disability) whenever a disability or second exceptionality is suspected in a gifted child or when students identified with a disability show signs of advanced reasoning, creativity or problem solving" (NAGC 2013).

Schools typically look for below-average or far-below-average performance when they test for problems with learning. However, the advanced reasoning ability of many 2e individuals, together with effort and support from their families and teachers, allows them to perform at an average level or at grade level in spite of a learning disability. Testing allows clinical and education professionals to look at measured strengths and measured weaknesses as well as relative weaknesses among abilities and within abilities. Testing can be done by the school at a parent's or teacher's request, by a clinical professional privately, or at a psychological assessment center. Ahmad's story shows how testing can be helpful.

• •

AHMAD, a bright, sensitive, kind-hearted, and thoughtful nine-year-old, was born in the United States shortly after his family arrived. His schooling has been entirely in US schools. The family speaks Arabic at home, and Ahmad speaks English fluently; he is solidly bilingual. He is creative, enjoys building, and has a great sense of humor. In school, he is hardworking, enjoyable to be around, and eager to participate in class discussions. Yet he is doing poorly in core subjects such as reading and is having difficulty maintaining focus, following through on a plan or assignment, and sitting still. He has trouble processing information fast enough, not only in the classroom but also at home and in extracurricular activities. Ahmad forgets to turn in completed assignments, has trouble following directions, does not like loud noises, worries excessively about unexpected fire drills, and has difficulty staying on track. He needs reminders to do basic tasks. He has trouble paying attention when doing homework and when learning plays during lacrosse practice. He becomes anxious at practice because it is a group setting. He prefers to have only one-to-one time with a friend.

• •

Ahmad (pseudonym for an actual client at an assessment clinic) underwent a cognitive test, an achievement test, a test of phonological processing, tests of visual and auditory attention, evaluations of executive functioning and auditory processing, and several questionnaires related to mood, behavior, and processing. The comprehensive evaluation revealed cognitive abilities and math skills in the highly gifted range (above the 99th percentile) as well as a pattern of weaknesses and significant challenges, which included phonological processing skills in the 1st to 15th percentiles, reading scores in the 5th to 10th percentiles, and writing scores in the 10th to 15th percentiles. His auditory processing scores were in the 1st to 16th percentiles, his visual processing scores were at the 9th percentile, and his visual-motor processing scores were in the 1st to 9th percentiles. Ahmad's attention and executive functioning scores also warranted concern. Based on these findings, as well as additional developmental and behavioral data, Ahmad was diagnosed as follows:

- ADHD combined presentation
- specific learning disability with impairment in reading and writing (dyslexia)
- developmental coordination disorder (dyspraxia/dysgraphia)
- other specified anxiety disorder

In addition, given Ahmad's low scores in auditory and visual processing, these areas of functioning were given "rule-out diagnoses" pending an evaluation from an audiologist and developmental optometrist. A rule-out diagnosis is an area of concern that will be further evaluated or monitored to determine whether it can be ruled out or warrants a full diagnosis.

So, what can be done with this information? Accommodations and interventions tailored to Ahmad's strengths and weaknesses can help him with many aspects of school life. Integrative and collaborative evaluation and treatment teams are the most effective approach. Those teams can develop a comprehensive treatment plan that considers Ahmad's challenges in totality and prioritizes and triages interventions.

In Ahmad's case, the plan might be to work closely with an auditory processing specialist to determine the best treatment for his auditory processing challenges. An educational therapist could help develop a multisensory approach to remediate Ahmad's current reading and writing limitations. He would also be referred to a developmental optometrist for a visual processing evaluation to determine whether he fits diagnoses such as convergence insufficiency (eyes have difficulty working together to decode letters and numbers and follow words smoothly), to be addressed with vision therapy. He also would see an occupational therapist, who can assess visual-motor (paper and pencil tasks; handwriting) and sensory processing (sensitivity to sound and noise) challenges and recommend therapy and accommodations. Ahmad's attention and executive functioning challenges can be monitored to determine if medication is needed, in addition to increasing structure and academic support. Finally Ahmad's school counselor should be made aware of his understandable stress, so that the counselor can work with him on relaxation exercises for stress reduction. The team can develop an IEP at school that might include daily academic support in a resource room as well as classroom accommodations for his various challenges (placing him in an advanced math group; inviting him to join a table group of peers with similar intellectual abilities; reduced writing and note-taking; extended time for tests; taking tests in a quiet setting; audio books; and oral reports, digital slideshows, and projects to show knowledge). Ahmad's anxiety is likely to decrease with these interventions and accommodations.

INTELLIGENCE TESTING WITH THE WISC-V

The Wechsler Intelligence Scale for Children, 5th Edition (WISC-V), is the most commonly used measure of IQ. Many states use the WISC-V Full Scale IQ score (a composite score) to determine eligibility for a gifted-education program. When Barbara Gilman and Dan were cochairing NAGC's Assessments of Giftedness Special Interest Group, they conducted a study that involved several US assessment sites, including the Summit Center in California and the Gifted Development Center in Colorado. They found significant discrepancies in domain (specific areas) scores for gifted and twice-exceptional youth, particularly in working memory (ability to hold and recall information) and processing speed (rate of visual-motor information processing). These large discrepancies resulted in a reduced Full Scale IQ score, which might preclude identifying and serving gifted and 2e students. To more effectively and fairly identify these students, the group recommended that "expanded index and composite scores on the WISC-V, such as the General Ability Index (GAI), Expanded General Ability Index (EGAI), Expanded Fluid Index (EFI), Verbal Expanded Crystallized Index (VECI), and Nonverbal Index (NVI)" be used in addition to the Full Scale IQ, which has historically been used by gifted programs and school districts (National Association for Gifted Children 2018). In summary, giftedness and advanced ability can be identified from several components of the WISC-V, not just from the Full Scale IQ score. Using various composite scores is important both for practical application and for the well-being of 2e children and teens.

GOALS AND STRATEGIES

Arranging supportive services for any 2e child or teen, with well-being in mind, often requires persistence and creativity. Below, common goals of supportive services are listed in order from surviving to thriving:

- Keep the child emotionally intact.
- Help the child survive school.
- Help the child feel successful.
- Nurture a continued love of learning.
- Instill confidence.
- Help the child thrive in school and life by paying attention to the above.

These modest but crucial goals are often accomplished through an IEP or a Section 504 plan. In order to qualify for an IEP, children must have one of the following designations: specific learning disability, autism spectrum disorder, emotional disturbance, or other health impairment. When qualified, children receive pull-out support services in a specialized classroom for part of the day (according to severity of need) and accommodations in the regular classroom. If children are not eligible for services through an IEP, they may qualify for a 504 plan when they have a developmental issue such as ADHD, mild learning challenges, dysgraphia, anxiety, or any other challenge that affects their ability to perform in the classroom. Section 504 plans allow for classroom accommodations and modifications to mitigate the negative impact of the challenge (for example, less handwriting required, preferential seating, or extended time for tests). When developing a formal strategy (IEP or 504 plan) or an informal strategy (a collaborative discussion with a teacher to discuss some accommodations in the classroom that might be tried prior to seeking a 504 or IEP), it is essential to first consider a child's strengths, then to scaffold areas of challenge to facilitate growth (create steps with increasing complexity and incremental support), and finally to create conditions to facilitate success.

Assistive technology and multimedia resources can set students up for success, as can preferential seating, freedom of movement (standing, walking, stretching), and choice for assignment topics. Individualizing, modifying, and/or compacting the curriculum (to reduce quantity); extending deadlines; and using pretests and posttests to determine needed curriculum are also common accommodations. Less concretely, emphasizing learning from mistakes, encouraging effort (to help students develop a growth mindset—see chapter 10), and promoting self-advocacy can be helpful. None of these strategies preclude high standards and flexible structure.

For testing, it's important to determine an optimal time of day to test, consider whether endurance limits are likely, make sure the testing environment is quiet and/or offer earplugs, and be clear about expectations and grading through review sheets and pretesting. Allowing freedom of movement, scheduling breaks for long tests, and arranging extended time may be appropriate accommodations. Some additional accommodation strategies for test-taking follow here:

- offering multiple options for demonstrating mastery: projects, oral presentations, teaching others, papers, artwork, plays, written tests, or digital presentations

- offering choices for testing methods, such as a teacher or aide reading test questions orally to the student, and/or the student answering orally

- allowing use of an attached teacher-created response sheet on a computer when the test does not otherwise involve a computer

- grading progress and effort separately on a project

- allowing answers to be written on tests or in test booklets instead of on computer-read sheets to prevent errors when moving eyes from test to answer sheet

- offering credit for written work with incorrect spelling, punctuation, and grammar if the content is accurate, organized, and presented well

- making extra-credit options available

GUIDELINES

Gilman and Peters's (2018) general guidelines for identifying and serving 2e kids are summarized or combined below. Some of these guidelines reflect the NAGC position statement on comprehensive assessment for 2e kids (National Association for Gifted Children 2013):

- Pay attention to bright children whose families have expressed concern about their academic, social, or emotional development. Parents and guardians are quick to notice unusual development not seen in other family members or issues similar to those of a family member with a disability. A parent's right to request a formal evaluation exists regardless of whether the child's needs were or are being addressed by RTI.

- Consider that any child who shows unusual strengths and coexisting relative weaknesses or lack of motivation is potentially a 2e child who warrants additional review. *The child's performance need not be below grade level.*

- Comprehensive assessment by a qualified school psychologist and/or other specialists, using psychometrically sound tests, is essential when a second exceptionality is suspected in a gifted child, or when advanced reasoning, creativity, or problem-solving is evident in a child with an already identified disability.

- *Gifted with coexisting disabilities* or *twice-exceptional* are appropriate phrases to describe a child for whom comprehensive assessment has confirmed these paradoxes. States should recognize that evidence for each half of the paradox should not be considered separately, but instead should be understood as interacting. If multiple measures are required as evidence, having more discretion and fewer mandated measures is helpful. Assessment by qualified outside professionals should be accepted as evidence of twice-exceptionality.

- IEPs guide school-based interventions and classroom and testing accommodations (for example, a student with debilitating anxiety taking tests in a quiet room, or a student with dyslexia having extra time for tests). A 504 plan is for modifications, potentially with consideration for both weaknesses and strengths (for example, fewer written responses, but not less rigor, for a gifted student with dysgraphia or a hand injury, or only the most challenging math problems). *A formal IEP or 504 plan provides crucial history when requesting accommodations on the SAT or ACT, or for assessments for service academies, or in college,* for example. An IEP or 504 plan also establishes a baseline of learning or processing challenges when changing schools (elementary to middle school to high school) or school districts.

- A classroom learning plan should emphasize strengths first and weaknesses second. Some examples of noncognitive strengths are leadership, communication, creativity, and talents in the visual and performing arts.

- According to federal legal guidelines, special education is not limited to measured low performance. A gifted student may have a learning disability and need support for writing, reading, speaking, organizing, social skills, or calming, for example (Musgrove 2012, 2013).

- Besides below-grade-level performance, discrepant performance across academic areas should be considered, as well as family reports of significant differences between learning and achievement in school and outside of school.

- Gifted-education specialists should be involved in planning RTI interventions for gifted or 2e students, since the most effective interventions take both exceptionalities into account and continue as long as the child progresses.

- In-service training can improve recognition of and services for twice-exceptionality.

- The US Department of Education Office for Civil Rights can provide information about 504 plans, and civil rights attorneys are available for staff training and parent questions. (For more information, see ed.gov/about/offices/list/ocr/docs/504-resource -guide-201612.pdf.)

WELL-BEING

Perhaps the most important words in the 2e CoP definition are "ensure the child's . . . social-emotional well-being." Bright kids have particular challenges and stressors due to their abilities and characteristics, such as intensity, heightened sensitivity, and asynchronous development. Twice-exceptionality may exacerbate these challenges and stressors.

It is the responsibility of caring adults, including parents and teachers, to try to understand the complex behaviors and emotions of 2e kids. When these are understood, a plan is then needed for providing differentiated curriculum for the advanced abilities, and intervention and accommodation for the areas of challenge,

> Bright kids have particular challenges and stressors due to their abilities and characteristics, such as intensity, heightened sensitivity, and asynchronous development. Twice-exceptionality may exacerbate these challenges and stressors.

including in the differentiated advanced curriculum. Next, 2e children need to learn about their strengths and challenges in age-appropriate ways so that they can make sense of their differentness from age peers at both ends of the bell curve of ability. Their understanding of their strengths and challenges can help them manage frustration when they face social and academic challenges that classmates may not face. This awareness can then lead to self-advocacy, which can increase over time. When they move into adulthood, 2e students will know what they need to be successful, how to ask for it, and how to obtain it. With this understanding and skill set, 2e children can become 2e adults who pursue an area of passion, lead with clear strengths, and understand what else they need for support and accommodation when they experience challenges.

POINTS TO PONDER

- Twice-exceptional individuals have both advanced abilities and areas of delayed development.
- Twice-exceptional profiles can be complex and vary from student to student.
- High abilities and areas of challenge can mask each other.
- Invested adults can identify patterns of inconsistent, puzzling performance.
- Comprehensive assessment is needed to understand patterns of 2e students' strengths and challenges.
- Twice-exceptional students require a formal individualized plan (IEP or 504 plan) to ensure differentiated services that fit their advanced abilities, and accommodations or modifications that offer support in areas of weakness.

Worrying

TEN-YEAR-OLD Sofia has difficulty falling asleep; she's unable to close the curtain on her active brain. Her parents and siblings come with her to family therapy. When asked to describe typical bedtime rituals, Mom says she lingers with Sofia, sometimes for half an hour, reassuring her over and over that there's nothing to worry about. After exploring possible contributors to anxiety and sleep challenges, including how Sofia feels at bedtime and prepares for it, counselor and family discover that Mom's repeated "nothing to be afraid of" actually increases Sofia's anxiety because it suggests that there might really be something to fear. Mom reveals that she had sleep problems at Sofia's age, because of family trauma, and she wants to protect her children from poor sleep. In an aha moment, Mom realizes she is contributing to what she wants to prevent. When she changes her behavior, bedtime quickly becomes easier for everyone. No more lingering, and no more replaying Mom's own fears nightly.

. . . .

GRADY, age nine, is known as a precocious thinker at school. But he struggles with math, and struggling academically is a new and frightening experience for him. He is usually quiet and compliant at school and on weekends, but at home after school, he terrorizes his little brother and the dog. The family arranges to come to counseling after Grady punches his fist through the drywall in the basement playroom. Cooperative and thoughtful, they describe the timing of, and their feelings during, Grady's violent outbursts. Grady says he worries about math homework, which he "hates," and it needs to be done before supper. The family connects the tantrums to Grady's struggles with math. Grady likes to swim, so Dad, a teacher, arranges for Grady to use the high school's pool daily for twenty minutes before the swim team needs it. On her way home from work, Mom drops off Grady to be with Dad. The intense activity helps him manage his anxiety about math and calmly do his homework. Creating a mantra to help him feel confident about math homework also seems to help.

. . . .

These vignettes reflect a systems approach for resolving excessive worrying, one that we are likely to use in a counseling setting when the complex interaction of a family or other group (perhaps within a larger system) may be contributing to a problem but could also be part of a solution. We have found that several additional therapeutic approaches can be helpful with high-ability clients, depending on concerns presented. Some are detailed in this chapter, not only to raise awareness in parents and teachers about how therapists might address concerns in young clients, after carefully gathering pertinent information, but also to provoke thought in clinical professionals themselves. Some cognitive behavioral and mindfulness strategies, designed for parents and teachers, are described later in this chapter. Approaches are effective only if clients believe they are meaningful and not just quick, one-size-fits-all fixes. Approaches need to make sense cognitively and resonate personally, including with children.

As discussed in chapter 2, bright children and teens tend to have intensities and sensitivities, also known as overexcitabilities; they are especially responsive to their emotions and thoughts and to sensory environmental stimuli. These kids are also able to consider how life *should* be and are often frustrated and discouraged when the ideal is not possible. In our clinical work, we have seen that characteristics such as the following can allow worry and anxiety to rule:

- ability to understand emotional and cognitive nuances
- unusual emotional depth
- abstract, complex, and/or insightful thinking
- idealism, especially with sensitivity about fairness
- silent preoccupation with their own thoughts
- complex concerns, leading to unsettling questions, which generate more worries
- highly developed curiosity
- divergent, outside-the-box thinking

Having advanced, nuanced thinking can lead to distress in general and anxiety in particular. In Dan's work with bright kids, many—if not most—of his clients experience mild to severe levels of anxiety. Sometimes the anxiety is primary, meaning it is the main and most distressing reason for coming to counseling. Sometimes the anxiety is secondary, meaning it is the result of something else, such as a poor fit at school, a learning or processing disorder, or being bullied or otherwise harassed. Whether primary or secondary, a pattern of anxiety can have a negative effect on a bright child or teen.

One boy in particular had great impact on Dan. He was in middle school, highly gifted, with logical, engineering-type strengths. His mother described his intense anxiety attacks when at Boy Scout camp, sleepovers, and other unfamiliar places. Dan tried many therapeutic approaches to help the boy reduce his anxiety, but unless he was in the middle of an attack, the boy did not believe he actually had anxiety concerns. The boy eventually attended Camp Summit, the camp for gifted kids that Dan cofounded. Dan witnessed an anxiety attack when the boy's parents were leaving. He was glad he saw it and looked forward to helping his client understand the experience in their next session.

The next week, when Dan met with the boy, the boy had no recollection of the anxiety attack. He could not describe it or provide any information about it. Dan picked up the plastic brain on his desk and asked, "Do you know how anxiety works in our brain and body?" The boy said, "No." Dan explained the fight-or-flight response in detail and noticed a new level of engagement in the boy. The next day, the boy's mother said in an email, "I don't know what you guys talked about yesterday, but he said it was the most helpful session he has ever had with you." Dan noted that it wasn't any of his fancy therapy tools that had worked; what was effective with this gifted client was helping him understand how his brain and body worked and using this *knowledge* to manage his fears.

Since this experience, Dan has routinely explained how anxiety works in the human brain and body, adding that tool to his menu of helpful approaches. His books *Make Your Worrier a Warrior* (for adults), *From Worrier to Warrior* (for older kids and teens) and *The Warrior Workbook* (for children) are based on clinical experiences like these. Teaching about the fight-or-flight response helps kids understand whether the "tiger" they believe is chasing them is real or fake. (See "Real Tiger or Paper Tiger?" on page 122.) This awareness is important for managing anxiety and fear and developing resilience. Providing bright kids with information and tools helps them grow and develop in healthy ways. One of the main strengths of bright children and teens is their ability to learn and apply information. Respecting both intellect and emotion is important when working with bright kids.

The situations listed below may be worrisome for any bright child or teen. However, Dan has found that, because of learning, processing, and/or developmental disabilities, 2e kids (see chapter 6) are often particularly anxious about one or more of these challenges, depending on their clinical profile:

- writing
- reading
- taking tests
- showing academic competence and mastery in ways acceptable to teachers
- public speaking
- completing schoolwork
- turning in classroom assignments
- meeting new people

- behaving in socially appropriate ways
- participating in sports
- self-advocating, being assertive, and attempting new activities
- driving a car
- applying for a job
- leaving for college
- transitioning into college

THE WORRY MONSTER

The Worry Monster idea comes from a narrative therapeutic approach, in which clients rewrite the narrative about their problem and about themselves. A key feature of this approach is to externalize the problem, creating separation between person and problem and creating space to strategize. The following questions might be helpful to start this process:

- "What does worry do for you?"
- "What does worry look like?"
- "What does worry tell you?"
- "How do you know when worry has sneaked in?"

Listing worries helps kids externalize what triggers their fears by making them visible on paper. One day, Dan was working with a bright girl who was courageously listing all her worries, and she was visibly scared. He asked her, "Do you want to see a picture of the pretend thing that is making you afraid and is bullying you?" "Yes," she replied nervously. Dan took out an illustration of a goofy green monster and said, "This is it. This is the bully that's messing with you." She responded, "He's dorky looking! He's not scary at all!" Her mother and Dan could immediately see the space created between her worries and herself and the instant improvement in her confidence. She took the picture home, put it on her bulletin board, and stuck pins into it whenever she had a victory over the monster. Her mother took a photo of the Worry Monster for the girl's phone wallpaper to remind her that worries are basically just a dorky bully who is a jerk.

The Worry Monster approach may sound as if it applies only to young children. However, Dan has found the concept to be effective with teens and adults as well. Some older teens and adults change the monster's name to something more appropriate for their age. The key is to label the entity as something or someone separate from the individual.

Jean has used a small figurine of an animal or human to externalize the problem of worrying (or another problem) for both children and teens. When she introduces it, she refers to it as a "he" or "she" or "it" and asks the client for a description of situations and feelings that make the figure grow "gigantic" at school or home. She also asks how big the problem is—and for whom it is a problem. (For example, it might be a bigger problem for a parent or sibling or teacher than for the child or teen.) She might ask what the client has tried to make the problem smaller.

Almost invariably, the client quickly begins to use the same pronoun Jean used, moving the problem from internal to external and potentially making it more manageable. At some point, Jean might say, "You're not just one big blob of anxiety (or anger or bad temper or underachievement). You're much more than that. This is just something you happen to be struggling with." At the end of the session, the client might give the figure a name. At later sessions, Jean might ask, "So, how big did (name) get last week (moving hands outward or upward)?" If smaller than usual: "How did you accomplish that? How were you able to make (name) smaller?" If bigger than usual: "How was (name) able to do that? How do you feel about that change?" These questions apply regardless of increase or decrease, because they are meant to help the client feel some power and control over the problem.

Jean may hide the figure behind a book during part of a meeting, asking the client how it feels to have it out of sight, and later asking if it's okay to bring it out again and talk about it. Externalizing a problem enables the child or teen to put it at arm's length, and not allow it to dominate. An externalized problem can be examined somewhat objectively. Then counselor and client can collaborate, strategize, and celebrate small victories.

Jean and a colleague once did a study of an elementary school counselor who used this strategy ("you have a problem to solve") almost exclusively to help the nearly five hundred kids in the school address social and other problems. One program component was organizing brief, small ad hoc classroom panels of children to address a real problem reported by the teacher (for example, a new girl in the class who feels lonely or someone feeling anxiety about bullying at recess) and to assist with ongoing instruction for all students about how to make the problem bigger or smaller. Always there was an empty chair in the panel for anyone in class who had some thoughts on the situation. Those who spoke individually then returned to their desks, and the discussion continued. Kids in the school learned to resolve their own problems, and playground combatants self-reported their conflicts and used a small room in the office area to "talk it out" by themselves, guided by a brief script. Jean concluded that this approach is applicable across all ability levels and circumstances— because most school problems, including anxiety, have a social component.

TYPES OF ANXIETY AND WORRY

Dan often uses a scene from the classic movie *The Wizard of Oz* as a metaphor to help kids see how understanding their worries can weaken them. Toward the end of the movie, Dorothy and her friends are approaching the wizard so that they can be granted their individual wishes. The wizard is loud and mean, saying he will not give them anything. Then Dorothy's dog Toto pulls back the curtain and exposes Oz the Great and Powerful as a simple man with gadgets who's been tricking everyone. Suddenly Dorothy and her friends perceive the wizard differently, and he loses his power. They become courageous and assertive.

Similarly, the more kids understand how the Worry Monster is bullying them, the more strategies they can figure out to counter it. They grow

> The more kids understand how the Worry Monster is bullying them, the more strategies they can figure out to counter it. They grow stronger, and the monster grows weaker.

stronger, and the monster grows weaker. To help kids reduce the Worry Monster's power, it is important for adults to know about the various types of anxiety the monster uses to confuse and distress people. The diagnostic manual of the American Psychiatric Association

(2013) elaborates further on the following types, except perfectionism, which is not included in the manual:

- **panic attack:** repeated adrenaline surges that result in physical symptoms and extreme fear
- **agoraphobia:** anxiety about being in places or situations from which escape might be difficult (or embarrassing) or in which help may not be available if a panic attack occurs
- **obsessive-compulsive disorder (OCD):** a condition in which a person experiences an anxiety-producing, intrusive, embarrassing, often persistent thought or idea (obsession) and/or a repetitive, intentional behavior (compulsion) intended to relieve the anxiety produced by an obsession
- **specific phobia:** a restrictive fear that is excessive, unreasonable, and triggered by the presence or anticipation of a specific object (such as snakes) or situation (such as public speaking)
- **social phobia:** a persistent fear of social or performance situations in which a person might be exposed to unfamiliar people or to scrutiny by others
- **post-traumatic stress disorder (PTSD):** a response of intense fear, helplessness, or horror, reexperienced after a traumatic event during which a person experienced, witnessed, or was confronted with events or situations that were life-threatening or involved serious injury
- **generalized anxiety disorder (GAD):** excessive and persistent anxiety and worry
- **separation anxiety disorder:** difficulty leaving parents (regardless of age)
- **perfectionism:** fear of failure; a constant state of anxiety about making errors, meeting extremely high standards, and perceiving excessive expectations and expecting negative criticisms from others

Simply growing up involves physical, emotional, and cognitive changes. Change means leaving behind something familiar and facing the unfamiliar ahead. Anxieties are therefore common after life events and during transitions, such as going to school for the first time, changing schools or neighborhoods, leaving for college, moving to a new home, parental separation or divorce, blending families, or accidents or illnesses that require major adjustments. For preteens and blossoming teens, developmental transitions likely involve new sexual feelings, troubling thoughts, thoughts about gender identity and sexual orientation, and no readily available person to talk with about these thoughts. Media bombardment may play a role in raising awareness of concerns related to sexuality, but peers also have an impact, including through bullying. In general, peer relationships are likely to change during adolescence, with new demands and concerns. Peers may become more important than parents as influencers.

When parents, guardians, teachers, and school counselors encourage planning for future education, bright and sensitive children and teens may feel anxious. They may be afraid of asking dumb questions about college; they may be concerned about finding the perfect college/university, major, career, or partner/spouse; and they may even be concerned about being a good parent, which they know is not a simple, tidy role. But most importantly, they know they are leaving childhood behind, a realization that may unsettle them. As they develop, they may also become increasingly fearful for their parents' safety, parents' relationship, or parents' employment. If parents share adult concerns with their adultlike bright children and teens, the kids' anxiety may increase.

Counselors and clinical psychologists do not have to diagnose a child to be effective as helpers. Instead, these professionals can recognize anxiety and consider whether and how much it is interfering with a child's or teen's life. If it is negatively affecting well-being, the strategies in this chapter might be useful. If parents or teachers notice that worrying is causing distress, we recommend that they consult a school or community counselor, or a counseling or clinical psychologist, preferably one who has experience working with bright kids. The responsibilities and time constraints of a school counselor's heavy student load and concerns about equity of services argue against doing long-term therapy with just a limited number of students, but the counselor might be willing to make some calls, inquiring about such expertise. Many school counselors keep updated lists of local mental health professionals and their specialty areas, based on website information and parents' or students' recommendations.

APPROACHES AND STRATEGIES

It is helpful to explain to a bright child that most worries stem from the Worry Monster tricking them into feeling uncomfortable or scared. When kids first feel an irrational worry, a small almond-shaped group of neurons in their brain called the amygdala goes off like a fire alarm, triggering the fight-or-flight response. This survival response is designed to keep them alive. Adrenaline is sent to their arms and legs to help them run or escape. However, this natural survival response causes a host of physiological symptoms, such as heavy breathing, stomach pain, lightheadedness, heart palpitations, a lump in the throat, clenched teeth, and cold hands. After an adult explains this response to a bright child, the body's reactions to their fears usually seem less mysterious and scary. This information tends to fascinate young children and helps them feel separate from the awful feelings. Children and teens can learn to identify which body symptoms they experience, such as stomachache or shortness of breath, which lets them know when the Worry Monster is visiting and they need to use some of the tools discussed in the rest of this chapter.

Cognitive Approach

The cognitive model of anxiety argues that thoughts determine emotions and behavior. In this model, anxious thoughts are always lies, distortions, irrational beliefs, exaggerations, or catastrophes. Cognitive-behavioral theorists and practitioners generally emphasize the following:

- **distressing thought:** "I am going to fail." "My mom is going to leave me." "What if they laugh at me?" "There will never be peace on Earth."

- **amygdala activation:** adrenaline surge, leading to physiological symptoms such as increased heart rate, sweating, muscle weakness, difficulty swallowing

- **behavioral response:** avoidance, emotional meltdown, disruptive behavior

Most worrisome and fearful thoughts begin with what-ifs like these:

- "What will I do if . . ."
- "What will people think if . . ."
- "What will happen if . . ."

To help bright children and teens counter worrisome, irrational thoughts about the future, adults can use the following steps to help kids challenge and replace those thoughts with more reasonable thoughts:

1. **Identify the thought:** "I am going to fail the test."

2. **Challenge the thought:** "Is it true that I fail tests? I didn't fail the last test."

3. **Modify or replace the thought:** "The test is going to be hard, but I'm prepared. I'm going to do fine. It's just a test."

Another helpful cognitive strategy is *positive self-talk,* which is simply talking oneself through a situation. For example, someone might say, "I can do this" or "It's going to be okay" or "It's just a game." Positive self-talk is a common, highly effective strategy that most people use regularly without realizing it. It is important to highlight this strategy as a skill—a tool in the toolbox for managing anxiety and worry.

Mindfulness

Mindfulness involves being aware in the present, rather than being stuck in the past or worrying about the future. The Dalai Lama said that those who live in the past tend toward depression because the past is gone and there is nothing they can do about it, and those who live in the future tend toward anxiety because the future hasn't happened and there is therefore nothing they can do about it (HH Dalai Lama and Cutler 2009). Thus, the primary goals in mindfulness are to focus on the present, let thoughts pass, and breathe. Students can use those three goals of mindfulness to manage worry and fear:

- **Stay present.** Being preoccupied with the future (the unknown) produces anxiety. Focus on what is happening in the current moment.

- **Notice anxious thoughts**, but do not believe them. Let them pass.
- **Breathe.** Focusing on breathing reduces adrenaline secretion and provides oxygen to the brain, with a calming effect.

Dan once was sitting with a high school client and writing down all her worries, as he had done during several previous sessions. After reviewing the list he said, "Do you realize that all the worries you have told me about over the years are in the future?" She thought a moment and then said, "They are! I never realized that, and they hardly ever happen!" Her mother, sitting next to her with a similar facial expression, said, "Mine are too!" Staying present and being aware of thoughts drifting to the past or the future is a simple, effective strategy for fighting the what-ifs.

Behavioral Interventions

A behavioral approach to reducing anxiety focuses on changing behavior rather than changing the thinking associated with a worry or fear. Changing a behavior changes thoughts and feelings. This approach is particularly helpful with young children who are not yet able to identify and describe their thinking. Some older children and teens, regardless of ability level, may also be unable to reflect on their thinking. Some behavioral strategies, adaptable for various age levels, follow here:

- **Fake it till you make it, or behave your way into feeling:** Do something and pretend that you like it. Pretending that you enjoy it can change your attitude toward it.

- **Predict pleasure:** Before doing something you don't want to do, predict on a scale of one to ten how much you will enjoy it. Rate the activity again afterward. A rating after the activity is often higher.

- **Rehearse what you want to conquer:** Do what you're afraid of (for example, riding in an elevator or crossing a bridge) over and over until it isn't scary anymore.

- **Systematically desensitize yourself:** Move in the direction you want, one step at a time, to overcome a challenge—a technique also known as baby steps, exposure, or success ladder. For example, if you're afraid of dogs, first look at pictures of dogs, then go to a park that usually has dogs and stay in the car, then leave the car and walk in the park far away from the dogs, and then pet a dog that has a calm temperament. The key is to practice each step until you don't feel afraid anymore, and then move on to the next fear. With each victory, you will be more confident and less scared.

> " Staying present and being aware of thoughts drifting to the past or the future is a simple, effective strategy for fighting the what-ifs.

Environmental Modifications at School

Besides altering thinking and behavior and building social and self-management skills, conversation during a therapy session, as strategies are applied, can help bright children and teens develop expressive language and feel and embrace emotions, lessening their distress. If external environmental stressors are contributing to worry and anxiety, making changes in the setting to remove or reduce these stressors can help reduce anxiety without encouraging the kids to simply avoid the stressor. Some examples of environmental modifications educators can make are these:

- identifying a go-to support person at school
- not requiring an oral answer in class or reading in front of the class
- giving more time to complete assignments
- reducing the amount of work required to show competence
- creating alternative ways to show competence or understanding
- allowing a student to sit in a place and position that feel comfortable
- reducing the number of Advanced Placement classes taken simultaneously

Many bright children, teens, and adults have benefitted from the approaches and strategies summarized in this section. Providing them with understanding, knowledge, and tools can be empowering for managing and overcoming worry and fear. Sometimes, however, the anxiety and fear are strong and entrenched, and professional consultation or counseling is needed. Discussing referral resources with kids and their families encourages the important coping skill of reaching out for help when a situation can't be resolved independently. Counselors, for example, can refer clients to pediatricians, psychiatrists, or other medical professionals with prescription privileges when they believe medication might be needed. A common perspective among helping professionals currently is that when mental health challenges warrant medical intervention, talk therapy *and* medication are more effective together than using either alone.

POINTS TO PONDER

- Understanding how brain and body react when they're scared helps kids monitor and manage fears.
- Externalizing the problem of worrying puts it at arm's length to examine and talk about.
- Being able to identify where they feel anxiety physically helps kids feel some control.

- Understanding that they can change anxious thinking into healthier thoughts can reduce anxiety and increase kids' ability to cope.

- Listing small steps toward conquering a worry or fear, starting with the least scary step, helps kids avoid feeling overwhelmed by the challenge.

- Practicing doing something the Worry Monster objects to gradually builds confidence.

- Collaboratively building a coping toolbox with go-to strategies helps kids be prepared for anxious thoughts.

Fearing Failure: Perfectionism

ELI, seven, is an intense, solemn, athletic boy. People who watch him play flag football marvel at his skill and leadership. They tell him he will have a great future. Most evenings, he runs sprints while his dad holds a stopwatch and critiques his form. Eli tells his mom that he needs to be a leader, that everyone on his team looks at him when something goes wrong because they know he will help them stay focused, calm, and encouraged. Lately, more and more often, when he makes a mistake on a test in school, he has a meltdown. His mom asks to meet with the counselor in Eli's school to discuss her concerns.

· ·

OLIVIA, fourteen, is an outstanding pianist and oboist. She is precociously knowledgeable about music and is nearly flawless as a student. Teachers notice that she never smiles, is usually alone, seems tense, and responds haltingly and suspiciously when they try to engage her in small talk before class begins. She has great respect for both of her private music teachers, who push her hard and only rarely give compliments. Her dad insists on high marks in classes and rarely speaks of anything else. He withholds praise and assurance. Her mom worries about Olivia's isolation and somber expression and makes an appointment with the school counselor.

· ·

When Jean asks parent audiences at her presentations what they have wished to talk about with a counselor, someone almost always mentions perfectionism. Both high-achieving and underachieving bright kids can struggle with perfectionism. Procrastination, high expectations of self and others, and assumptions that others expect a lot from them are all associated with perfectionism.

Perfectionism is more complex than just being fussy or tensely conscientious. Even articulate adults who acknowledge their own perfectionism might have difficulty explaining it. In this chapter, we respect that complexity.

Perfectionism is a complicated and controversial concept. According to Kristie Speirs Neumeister (2016), known for her studies of perfectionism, one concern is that researchers studying perfectionism usually study only high achievers—that is, children, teens, and college students identified as having exceptional ability at least partly because of outstanding academic performance. Academic underachievers with comparable intellectual ability are much more difficult to find and study (see chapters 4 and 5), but they too may be burdened by perfectionism. Bright kids with one or more learning disabilities (see chapter 6) are also probably not involved in studies of perfectionism but can indeed experience it. An additional concern is that definitions, measurement, and views of perfectionism vary widely among research studies.

Some scholars have concluded that perfectionism should be viewed on a continuum from "healthy" to "unhealthy," adaptive to maladaptive. If someone enjoys the pursuit of excellence, is not debilitatingly preoccupied with evaluation, does not react negatively to mistakes, and does not wither when facing challenges, these scholars view that as healthy perfectionism. On the flip side, constant anxiety about error or not meeting expectations reflects unhealthy perfectionism. That kind of perfectionism might also involve avoidance—of people, assignments, social comparisons, and evaluation.

Thomas Greenspon, a Minneapolis therapist specializing in high ability, objects to the notion of good and bad perfectionism, claiming that perfectionism always involves fear of failure. He makes this assertion about a perfectionistic person's emotional world:

> We are prone to misconstrue the perfectionism in highly successful perfectionistic people as "healthy" or "adaptive," and we are likely to confuse the many positive personality character- istics of perfectionistic people, such as conscientiousness, persistence, and dedication, with some kind of healthy perfectionism. Perfectionistic people, though, do not see their chronic, pervasive anxiety about mistakes as positive or healthy. (2016, 10)

WHAT PERFECTIONISM MIGHT LOOK LIKE

What perfectionism looks like varies from context to context and from person to person. Eli and Olivia, introduced at the outset of this chapter, are similar in their efforts to meet a tough taskmaster's high expectations. They are not familiar with the term *conditional* as it relates to approval, nor have they considered that unconditional love actually exists some- where. But conditional acceptance and respect, perceived to be granted only for "perfec- tion," dominate their experiences in an area of talent. Yet Eli and Olivia represent only a few aspects of perfectionism. A broader picture of perfectionism might include an older elementary child who stays up until 11:00 p.m. to double-check homework answers several times at an excruciatingly slow pace; a young child who cannot leave for school until both bedroom and closet are in perfect order; a young teen who drops out of an after-school interest club because the skills involved are "too hard"; and a high school athlete who cannot tolerate even a mild critique by a coach, resulting in tension at home after practices.

Some students submit no homework even when it is complete. When their teachers ask about the blank spaces in the gradebook, the students say the work is not good enough. Other students ask repeatedly for help with in-class opinion essays, adding, "I want to make sure it's what you want." Other varieties of perfectionism are seen in a teen who comes home daily with a long report of high-stress situations involving teachers shaming and blaming students for poor-quality work, or another student's parents saying, "Just do your best," interpreted as, "Be number one in my class."

Lisa Van Gemert, an educator and consultant specializing in gifted students, noted that people sometimes change what they are perfectionistic about. They may also behave paradoxically—for example, having a messy room, but putting unrealistic demands on themselves about a project. She observes that when perfectionism is situational, the extent of the problem may be minimized or missed (Van Gemert 2017).

Dan recalls meeting with Nafnati, a ninth-grader. Nafnati's middle school was highly academic and achievement oriented. She worried a lot, but always felt better when she checked her grades online and saw all A's. She spent more hours on homework than her peers did, but her parents helped her with it and supported her when she was anxious or had meltdowns. Her new high school was a competitive college-prep school, but it focused more on the whole child and growth and less on classroom achievement. It did not test as often nor record grades regularly. Nafnati became depressed and increasingly anxious. She said she had lost her coping strategy of checking her grades: "If I can't get all A's and see them, what's the point of going to school?" She left her high school to be homeschooled, saying her life had lost meaning. Her story illustrates that bright kids' sense of self-worth may rest solely on what they produce or achieve. Nafnati saw no purpose to learning without concrete assessment of it.

MORE THAN HIGH ACHIEVEMENT MATTERS

During their study of negative life events, Jean and her colleagues concluded a questionnaire with an open-ended question: "What should teachers understand about bright kids like you?" The participants' responses revealed that sensitivity to evaluation and criticism was a common problem. One student wrote, "Need gentle feedback." Another wrote, "We need unconditional acceptance. More than high achievement matters" (Peterson, Duncan, and Canady 2009).

WORKSHOPS AND SMALL-GROUP DISCUSSIONS: OPPORTUNITIES TO INQUIRE

When Jean conducted a workshop with 150 bright high school students in a small university city, Jean asked them to complete an informal, unpublished questionnaire about perfectionism, with scaled responses 1 to 10, 10 being highest. Items with extreme responses (8 to 10) are summarized here:

- 51 percent were highly self-critical.

- 32 percent were highly critical of others.

- 32 percent generally felt very inferior to others.

- 29 percent were highly self-critical when they made mistakes.

- 18 percent did not enjoy doing a task or project at all.

- 15 percent found it very difficult to begin something.

- 11 percent definitely did not play well (didn't know how to "just play," weren't comfortable with "just playing," didn't play much).

It might not be surprising that half of those bright teens were highly self-critical—or that nearly one-third were highly critical of others and hard on themselves when they made mistakes. However, other connecting links were surprising in their clarity:

- Feeling inferior and being self-critical.

- Kids who are concerned about evaluation have difficulty relaxing and enjoying a task.

- Kids who fear they can't meet their own or others' expectations might procrastinate with an assignment, an essay, or a project.

One speculation, about play, is that competitive kids who need to be "the best" or "win" find it difficult to play just for fun, either alone or with others, or to take time away from academic work and extracurricular activities to simply play.

When Jean facilitated weekly small-group discussions with high-ability middle-school students in the same city, she was concerned that nearly all of the five groups talked continually about their GPA (grade point average) during at least the first three meetings. While that preoccupation made sense in a university community, Jean noticed that they talked about their stellar academic performance with a sad weariness, not pride or bravado. The topics of the early meetings were stress, strengths and limitations, enjoyment and satisfaction, and identity—and yet the students talked tensely and at length about their grades. Only when later meeting topics required self-reflection and discussion of feelings and challenges related to growing up did the students relax, sit less stiffly, let their shoulders sag a little, and connect with each other about *non*academic life.

Based on her experiences with bright children and teens at several age levels, including during many years of small-group discussions, Jean concluded that kids struggling with perfectionism often have difficulty with the following:

- taking reasonable risks instead of playing it safe and needing to stay in control (social risks, safety risks, and academic risks)

- focusing on *being* (being comfortable with self, interested in learning about self, having an accurate sense of self and of others' perceptions, and being aware of personal strengths and limitations) more than on *doing* (accomplishment, performing, evaluation, and competition)

- setting reasonable standards and goals

- feeling satisfied—even with excellent work

- beginning, ending, or enjoying whatever needs to be done (due to fear of not being able to meet expectations, concern about not doing enough, or being overwhelmed by the stress of the situation)

- enjoying the process ("the trip"), instead of being preoccupied with the product ("the destination")

- enjoying the present moment, instead of worrying about the next hurdle

- accepting that mistakes are an inevitable part of life, not character flaws

- tolerating ambiguity; recognizing that there is usually more than just one way to do something

- accepting that, in most situations, having complete control over what happens is probably not possible or even desirable

- changing an all-or-nothing view of complicated situations (all bad or all good, all right or all wrong) or of assigned tasks ("If I can't do it perfectly, I won't do it at all.")

- not comparing self with others constantly

- revealing weaknesses or imperfections to someone else

- feeling done with good-quality work, and not doing it over and over to make it "perfect"

- feeling satisfied with situations that are not ideal; feeling low morale, stress, anxiety, and depression instead

- forming and maintaining peer relationships—because of unreasonable expectations of themselves and others

- accepting criticism

- imagining unconditional love—because they hear or imagine "conditions" on being loved

When Jean mentions these points in presentations at professional conferences or adult workshops about social and emotional development, they routinely generate good discussion. Usually several adult workshop participants or audience members remark that they realize they themselves are perfectionists and are modeling perfectionism for kids.

DEVELOPMENTAL PERSPECTIVES

Because researchers of perfectionism have focused mostly on college students and adults (not kids), parents, educators, and clinical professionals must base their perspectives about kids on what they observe. They likely associate perfectionism with bright, talented kids because the latter are able to perform at high levels and consider complex ideas. But those invested adults might also notice that when schoolwork is not challenging, and these kids are successful in whatever they try, they may begin to avoid situations where they are not sure they can succeed—common among perfectionistic individuals. Competitive peers and perfectionistic teachers may exacerbate perfectionism, which may already be entrenched because some bright kids believe they must be "best." They may also set unreasonable standards for themselves as a result of spending a lot of time with older peers and adults. With asynchronous development (see chapter 2), perfectionistic young children may not have the advanced hand and finger skills needed for tasks they think they should be able to master.

Regardless of age, perfectionism is potentially detrimental socially (preoccupation with others' evaluation or one's own unreasonable expectations of others; extreme self-criticism and constrained behaviors). In contrast, if comfortable synergy develops over shared interests and high goals, and interaction is mutually beneficial, comfortable, satisfying, and not preoccupied with error or negative competitiveness, then perfectionism likely doesn't have a role in such relationships.

Schuler: Summarizing Perfectionism Research

Patricia Schuler (2002), a psychologist focused on concerns related to high ability, noted that perfectionism is a major counseling concern for gifted children and teens. Among several points in her summary of perfectionism research, she wrote that individuals with perfectionistic tendencies measure self-worth by accomplishment and productivity but have difficulty feeling satisfaction from performance. Perfectionism has also been associated with depression, migraines, obsessive-compulsive disorder (OCD), underachievement, procrastination, and negative effects on career. Some scholars believe that the pressures of perfectionism come from within, while others blame perfectionistic parents who value performance more than learning. Early, intense academic training and comments from adults about being "perfect" also might contribute to perfectionism.

Greenspon: Expectations, Anxiety, and Mistakes

Greenspon offers a useful definition of perfectionism: "an intense desire for perfection and intense fear of imperfection" (2016, 10). He emphasizes understanding the emotions involved in perfectionism, not just the behaviors. When bright kids have a good fit with classroom academics, school is an opportunity for perfection, within their control. In fact, high achievement may be the one aspect of a complicated life that is controllable. Perfectionism may therefore be limited to school—or be more pervasive.

Mistakes can threaten connection to others. If high-ability kids feel judged or disliked, and adults are happy only when these kids are highly successful, mistakes may be associated with shame, being defective, being rejected by people who matter, being unacceptable to others, and feeling isolated. Unfortunately, people who struggle with perfectionism often have difficulty receiving guidance to counter perfectionism because that guidance adds to the felt burden of expectations.

Conscientious effort, commitment to doing things well, and a focus on personal growth are not associated with perfectionism. However, even when conscientiousness, persistence, and dedication result in excellence, anxiety about mistakes may be the dominant emotion. Perfectionism is meant to counter the anxiety, according to Greenspon.

A drive from within, in addition to internal and external high expectations, may contribute to problematic perfectionism. Bright kids who are highly committed, award-focused, quiet, hesitant, or procrastinating may actually be struggling with perfectionism. Elite athletes and musicians may have no sense of self beyond their extreme capability. Their mental health may be at risk when they eventually pause to self-reflect, are perceived to be past their prime, retire in their twenties, and have had little or no guidance except as related to high performance (Grobman 2006; Rapkin 2020).

Krafchek: A Study of Disordered Eating

The focus of a recent interview-based doctoral study of high-achieving females was on disordered eating (Krafchek and Kronborg 2018, 2019). However, several findings are of interest here, since perfectionism and control are often associated with this focus. One finding was that the role of academic success shifted—from source of self-worth and positive emotions to both coping strategy and stressor. This research epitomizes the value of in-depth exploration of the social and emotional world of bright high achievers.

Ideally, children feel secure at home, with parents and guardians giving positive feedback for personal qualities and successes. Teachers and peers at school communicate support and approval. Schoolwork, done well, also contributes to self-worth. Family and school are therefore sources of self-worth, and children feel control, confidence, and positive emotions. However, if a life event or situation, such as parental divorce, family relocation, tragedy, or an unsupportive teacher, interrupts that sense of control and those positive emotions, academic achievement may become the new source of self-worth, a means of coping, but eventually a source of high stress.

In the Krafchek study, teacher bullying, sarcasm, and humiliation about minor mistakes altered the landscape for some participants. When teachers no longer offered praise, the girls interpreted that change as negative feedback. They hid their distress and did not tell a parent or guardian about the offending teachers. An especially difficult class or several challenging classes threatened security and predictability. In this study, eating became a means of problem-solving and control when at least three major stressful events had occurred, even over ten years, and previous coping strategies were no longer effective.

Surprisingly, when Krafchek asked participants about perfectionism, it was not of interest to them. It did not seem to be the main contributor to eating problems; nor were weight and body dissatisfaction and parental behaviors, which educators and clinical professionals commonly assume are contributors. Instead, it was cumulative stress that led to self-doubt and negative emotions, and participants then pursued self-worth and positive emotions to protect their sense of themselves. Pertinent to perfectionism, they knew how to perform well academically and could predict outcomes and feel control. They applied extreme self-regulation. But it was many stressors that ultimately led to disordered eating. Regarding common understandings of perfectionism, the girls were focused on high standards, but were not preoccupied with avoiding mistakes. Instead, they were vulnerable to eating problems when negative experiences happened in an area tied to their self-worth. The findings in this study, challenging some common assumptions, increase understanding of perfectionism by *not* connecting it to eating disorders and should be explored further.

STRATEGIES AND APPROACHES

Among many possible counseling strategies for addressing perfectionism, we offer three to conclude this chapter: psychoeducation, small-group discussion, and activities. These three are possible in most therapeutic contexts, and parents and teachers can make use of them as well.

Psychoeducation

Individuals who experience perfectionism often don't know what they are experiencing. They are used to thinking one way—*their* way—about themselves and the world. Just as it is important to inform a bright person about how their brain and body interact to generate the fight-or-flight response, it is crucial to

Perfectionism is usually related to fear of failing and extremely high personal expectations that are difficult to meet, hard to sustain, and feel good for only a moment before the next challenge arrives.

educate bright children and teens about perfectionism. Perfectionism is usually related to fear of failing and extremely high personal expectations that are difficult to meet, hard to sustain, and feel good for only a moment before the next challenge arrives.

One strategy for countering perfectionism clinically is to collaboratively distinguish among perfectionism (or fear of failure) and striving for excellence (or taking reasonable risks to create excellence) (Adderholt, Johnson, and Levy 2015; Greenspon 2016; Peters 2013a, 2013b). The latter involves discovering personal strengths and capabilities through taking those risks, while accepting that there will be mistakes and errors in judgment along the way. Many bright children and teens have talented and accomplished young and older adults nearby to emulate, and these adults have likely experienced failures en route to excellence. "Perfect" lives are not perfect, yet they can be realistic exemplars, worthy of emulation. Using the ideas in this paragraph as discussion prompts, adults can provoke helpful interaction with kids about perfectionism.

Dan usually keeps the following guidance in mind when he's working with individual children or teens struggling with perfectionistic thinking and behavior:

- Help them take a reasonable risk: try something new. Give them permission not to do it well.

- Help them practice failing. In fact, *prescribe* failure when the stakes are low.

- Help them understand that there are many ways to do a task.

- Help them focus on having fun versus winning and being "best."

- Pay attention to what they care about. Help them learn to prioritize, take time to reflect on the value of mistakes and relaxation, and take the risk of pursuing strong interests.

- Emphasize effort and determination (instead of being "smart"); deemphasize the assumption that everything has to be done well. (For more on this approach, see Carol Dweck's perspectives on mindset presented in chapter 10.)

Discussion

If perfectionism is a common problem in a group of adolescents, they might brainstorm strategies like the following for combatting perfectionism. The following suggestions come from Jean's 2020 book *Get Gifted Students Talking*:

- Be average for a day. Give yourself permission to be messy, late, incomplete, imperfect.

- Become involved in activities that are not graded—and enjoy them. Consider a "process" approach to life—that is, viewing life as a journey. Be involved in something with no end or product in mind.

- Take a risk. Sign up for a class that has a reputation for being challenging. Smile and start a conversation with someone you don't know. Do an assignment or study for a test without overdoing it. Alter your morning routine. Start a day without a plan.

- Give yourself permission to make at least three mistakes a day. Smile at them.

- Plan less compulsively.

- Stop using the words *should* and *I have to*.

- Share a weakness or limitation during a conversation with a friend. Your friend will not think less of you.

- Acknowledge that your self-expectations might be unrealistic and unreasonable.

- Find out more about perfectionism.

- Think about what might contribute to your perfectionism. Comments heard at home or school? Wanting approval? Fearing disapproval? A hard-wired perfectionistic personality?

- Savor your past accomplishments. Savor the present moment.

- Ask friends to help you overcome your perfectionism by giving you a signal when they notice it.

- Tell yourself repeatedly that it's okay to be less than perfect.

- Laugh at yourself—and at your perfectionism.

In addition to these strategies, the approach in chapter 7 of using a figurine to represent the problem can be effective at home or in a counseling session as a reminder to intentionally monitor and note progress toward managing the size of the problem of perfectionism.

Greenspon uses open-ended questions like these to facilitate conversation and encourage self-reflection:

- "What makes being perfect seem so important?"

- "How do you feel when you make a mistake?"

- "You seem nervous when you're answering a question. What are you feeling then?"

He also encourages invested adults to observe their own language when interacting with kids. Is it judgmental? Is the focus on what is done well or on what could be done better? Does the language imply that a mistake is not okay? Because children and teens absorb the messages and behavior of their parents and guardians, it is important for those adults to identify perfectionistic thinking and behavior in themselves, which they may be modeling unintentionally. They can teach their perfectionistic children and teens, and remind themselves as well, that sometimes good enough is good enough.

Adults can engage perfectionistic children and teens in dialogue, building a relationship with them, even if only (as teachers, for example) to check in with them casually, routinely. In general, adults should focus on who kids *are*, not on what they *do*. Noticing their strengths (such as effort, persistence, kindness, and thoughtfulness) can help bright kids build a safe, secure base. Feeling accepted and connected, perfectionistic youth may begin to take appropriate social and academic risks. When teachers notice anxiety about assignments, they might check with parents or guardians, who might also be noticing anxiety. Online and print resources can provide psychoeducational information beyond what this chapter offers.

Activities

The following questions might be included in an activity that engages middle and high school students about concepts included in this chapter, without "right" or "wrong" evaluation. The intent is that the content comes from them, not from the discussion leader:

1. Some kids with high ability struggle with perfectionism. What comes to mind when you hear the word *perfectionism*?

2. What might be a clue that it's a problem—that someone needs help to combat perfectionism?

3. Some people say perfectionism is always bad. Others say perfectionism varies—on a continuum line between helpful and harmful. What do you think about these two views? On a scale of 1 to 10, with 10 representing extreme perfectionism, where might you be on a continuum of perfectionistic behavior, thoughts, and feelings?

4. Is there a difference between "striving for excellence" and "perfectionism"? What are your thoughts about this distinction?

5. Some people believe perfectionism is okay if it doesn't hurt your health, schoolwork, or relationships. What is your opinion about this view?

6. Some people say that perfectionists can't enjoy the trip because they're preoccupied with the destination. What do you think this metaphor is referring to?

7. Some people believe that perfectionism is about wanting to avoid mistakes. What do you think about that view?

8. A therapist-scholar believes that perfectionism always means fear of failure. What is your opinion of that claim?

9. Some people say that perfectionists avoid taking risks because they like to stay in control and know what to expect. If that is true, what kinds of risks might they avoid in school? In life? At home? What are some risks you take or are likely to take in the future? What are some risks you are unlikely to take?

For younger children, an activity might include the following questions. Jean has also used these questions with teens and adults (with the title "How Perfect Do I Need to Be?") to provoke self-reflection and discussion, with good results.

Where do I care about having things "perfect"?

❏ my hair
❏ my homework
❏ my clothes
❏ my closet
❏ my storage drawers
❏ being good
❏ my body
❏ my friendships
❏ getting good grades
❏ being clean
❏ sports
❏ food

❏ being nice
❏ behaving
❏ writing or printing
❏ other people's behavior
❏ drawing
❏ colors matching
❏ games
❏ winning
❏ my room
❏ my pillow
❏ my bed
❏ my desk or locker at school

What might be good about wanting things to be "perfect"?
What might be bad about wanting things to be "perfect"?

POINTS TO PONDER

- Perfectionism takes many forms, though it often reflects fear of failure and high self-criticism.

- Perfectionism is often quiet and hidden.

- Bright students often have high internal standards that may be exacerbated by adult comments and expectations.

- Overcoming perfectionistic thinking takes targeted effort and practice.

- It is important for adults to be aware that they might be modeling perfectionistic thinking and behavior for their children or students.

- High achievers and bright underachievers can both be perfectionistic.

Feeling, Struggling, Hiding

NEELI, her two brothers, and their mom moved into the district several years ago. Her brothers were rebellious and noncompliant throughout middle and high school. Neeli has been an unremarkable student so far and is now starting another year of basic-level high school classes. The yearbook advisor is surprised when Neeli announces her wish to be a photographer—and she does good work, writing thoughtful copy for her carefully composed photos. The advisor encourages her to switch to a higher-level English class as soon as possible. In it Neeli's writing improves steadily, and she moves on to that teacher's advanced-level novels course in the second semester. Two days after she chooses James Agee's *A Death in the Family* as a student-option book, she returns the book and says, "I can't read this one." Puzzled, but seeing the distress in Neeli's face, the teacher asks to talk with her at the end of the day. "This book is what happened to me," she says. Quietly and tensely, Neeli describes what she saw at age seven from the back of the family camper: her dad, whom she adored, lying on the road, dead from a heart attack. In the days that followed, Neeli heard more than one adult say, "She's too young to understand." No one talked with her about her dad. Her mother was overwhelmed, the boys ran wild, and Neeli retreated—until she began to read Agee's book. Neeli and her teacher set aside twenty minutes on Fridays to talk before first-hour classes begin. Healing and multilayered learning happen, transforming Neeli's self-concept.

. . . .

Because comparative studies are rare and samples are often limited and skewed (for example, high achievers only, clinical cases only, diagnosed only, residential schools or summer programs only), any general claim about the mental health of bright kids should be considered with caution. However, a rare, recent study of 3,715 adult American Mensa members (measured intelligence at or above the 98th percentile, ages eighteen to ninety-one), with comparison data available from national health surveys, is thought-provoking (Karpinski et al. 2018). Findings suggest that the overexcitabilities associated with high intellectual capacity may put high-IQ *adults* at relatively higher risk for psychological disorders. The researchers could not say whether, how, and to what extent bright kids in general, or those identified for school programs, experience these mental health concerns. However, the findings do relate to the concept of overexcitabilities discussed in chapter 2 and can also be considered in relation to a CDC report that 13 to 20 percent of US children ages three to seventeen experience a mental disorder in a given

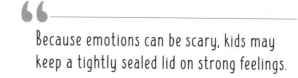

Because emotions can be scary, kids may keep a tightly sealed lid on strong feelings.

year (Perou et al. 2013). Assumedly, though that statistic represents as many as one in five children, the mental health of the rest, like of the vast majority of bright kids, does not meet criteria for a mental disorder.

Nonetheless, those findings also reflect what we have observed in our clinical work with bright individuals and families. During small-group discussions in school and summer programs, in therapy sessions, and in classroom essays, bright kids have taught us about their complicated feelings and frightening internal struggles. In several of Jean's studies of high-ability kids, participants indicated that they hid their struggles. Adults need to be alert for evidence of concerns.

In this chapter we present our perspectives about bright kids' social and emotional challenges. We suggest reasons for hiding distress and offer some strategies for helping these kids come out of hiding. Neeli's emotions and her capable mind were hidden for many years. That kind of hiding, rarely discussed in the field, is our main focus here.

THE INTERNAL WORLD

Bright kids vary widely not only in type and combination of intellectual and other strengths, but also in personality, interests, developmental tempo, and personal circumstances. They are difficult to categorize. Their internal world, where feelings reside, is often difficult for peers and adults to access—maybe even for the bright kids themselves. Because emotions can be scary, and families might express them only violently (if at all), kids may keep a tightly sealed lid on strong feelings. Regardless of whether their external behavior suggests happy, satisfied kids who are comfortable with themselves, easy to be around, and invested in learning and activities—or dissatisfied kids who are disengaged, explosive, rebellious, and scarred by life— they can have significant concerns. Because of characteristics associated with high ability, positive and negative extremes of behavior might reflect distress of similar intensity.

Psychologist Frank Main conducted a memorable workshop for district gifted-education teachers when Jean was new in the field. When he was asked whether individuals with exceptional ability have better mental health than others, as some scholars were claiming, he noted that, in his clinical view, bright people tend to "skip over" (perhaps ignoring, hiding, managing, and not seeking help for) "garden-variety" concerns, coming to the attention of educators and clinical professionals only when problems have become full-blown mental health issues. He said he generally didn't see gifted individuals with uncomplicated concerns in his office. He didn't refer to characteristics associated with exceptional ability, but those might explain what he saw clinically. Those characteristics can exacerbate expected challenges during individual and family developmental transitions and in the aftermath of negative life events.

Bright kids and their parents might view high stress as "normal," and concerns might be neither obvious nor accurately identified. If they are able to control their behavior and manage their public image, bright kids may not take the risk of talking about their concerns either at school or at home. With nimble minds and verbal strengths, they can probably maintain control with banter, clever repartee, arguing, and debating, thereby avoiding social risk-taking and emotional vulnerability and deflecting questions about feelings when conversations become personal.

FEELING

Despite their apparent self-control, bright kids may feel "crazy" inside because of confusing, unsettling emotions. Those uncomfortable emotions may be intensified by abilities and asynchronous development (see chapter 2). These kids' place on the bell curve of intellectual ability makes them different from all but a few of their age peers. Being different in the eyes of peers and teachers is uncomfortable for many students.

More specific social and emotional concerns might also be unsettling, affecting sleep, eating, social ease, and vision of the future:

- They might be recent immigrants and/or in a cultural minority, seeing negative social media posts or news commentary about their country of origin or culture and hearing taunts and slurs from hostile individuals at school and in the community.

- They might be wondering seriously about gender identity or sexual orientation even in elementary school. That timing was typical of half the participants in a study of gifted gay, lesbian, bisexual, and transgender young adults looking back at their school years (Peterson and Rischar 2000). Current media attention to gender identity and sexual orientation may help bright children and teens make sense of unsettling feelings. They might want to talk to someone specifically about feeling asexual (not attracted to anyone) or nonbinary (not fitting strict male-female distinctions), for example.

- They might worry that their lack of a good friend now means that finding mind-mates will be a lifelong challenge. (They are likely to find a comfortable fit with others as their education continues and as they establish careers involving like-minded colleagues.)

- They might worry that someone will find out that they are not as smart as they appear to be.

- They might experience depression deep enough that it affects most aspects of their life.

- They might, with angry despair, feel that they don't matter—and that "someone must pay."

STRUGGLING

Vague Sadness

Vague, unexplained sadness is common among bright kids. It is helpful to look at this sadness through a counseling lens. Characteristics associated with high ability may exacerbate kids' responses to life changes. But identifying what is contributing to a dull, gnawing sadness might be difficult, especially when parents, guardians, teachers, coaches, and others keep saying, "You have so many great things going for you." The following are among many possible experiences that can contribute to sadness:

- trauma

- altered peer relationships

- adjustments to an unfamiliar academic area

- transitioning from elementary to middle school, and from middle school to high school

- having multiple teachers instead of one main teacher

- frightening and discouraging TV news reports

- less attention and support from teachers than in the past

- becoming aware that a terrible personal situation won't be better in the future

Change Means Loss

Even small changes in life can provoke feelings of loss and sadness. But when families change in major ways, perhaps suddenly, or when health or financial concerns turn stable circumstances upside down, grief makes sense. A simple activity can frame developmental events as change and loss and address feelings of aloneness or differentness that may accompany them. Some of the following might be *selected and adapted* as a paper checklist for group discussion. The value is in learning that change and loss are common among age peers, not in the details, out of respect for family privacy. Kids can check items that apply to them and raise a hand for these during a go-around for each item. The leader can keep track of number of hands per item, and, at the end of the activity, the group might guess which experiences were most common and then comment about their thoughts and feelings during the activity. Wording appropriate for young children follows each item here.

- death of someone close or loss of a special friendship
  - » My aunt, who I liked a lot, died from the virus.
  - » This year my best friend is not my friend anymore.
- death of a pet
  - » My dog died.
  - » My cat is dying from cancer. I don't know what I'll do without her.

- a natural disaster
  - » Our home was wrecked in the big storm.
- a pandemic or epidemic
  - » We couldn't go to school or to the park or to visit my grandma.
- moving away from friends or friends moving away
  - » I moved to a different house and a different school.
  - » A good friend moved away.
  - » When we moved, I had to say good-bye to my best friend.
- loss of relationship with a sibling or parent
  - » When my dad got a new wife, I didn't see him very often.
  - » When my sister started eighth grade, she didn't pay attention to me anymore.
- losing trust in someone or something
  - » My mom and dad won't let me visit my uncle anymore because they can't trust him.
  - » I thought I'd always have a family to count on, but my brother's addiction changed everything, including my mom and stepdad's marriage.
- a serious illness or bad accident for myself or a family member
  - » My grandpa is in the hospital.
  - » My family was in a bad accident over the weekend. My mom and dad were hurt.
- a change in family structure and life
  - » My parents got a divorce. My mom married someone from a different town and lives there.
  - » My dad's job was cut.
  - » My brother went off to college.
- disappointment in someone significant
  - » I found out my favorite cousin has a drug problem.
  - » My oldest sister got sort of wild this year and is gone a lot.
- a traumatic experience
  - » Some kids cornered me in the locker room and took off my pants. A coach came in just in time.
  - » I was really sick for a long time. My family was scared for me.
  - » I was abused when I was five.

- loss of innocence, loss of childhood, loss of the past
  - » I didn't think my brother and his friends would get into trouble like that.
  - » My mom is sick a lot, and I have to take care of her every morning and after school.
  - » When we moved here, I started forgetting about where I used to live.
- loss of security, reputation, or safety
  - » She texted terrible things about me, and everyone believed her.
  - » When a boy in my class got that sickness, I kept thinking I'd get it.
- loss of position in family
  - » I used to be the oldest, but my mom got a new husband, with kids, and I'm not oldest now.
  - » I used to be my grandma's only grandchild, but then my brother was born.
- loss of a relied-upon strength
  - » I used to be really smart in math, but I'm having a lot of trouble with geometry.
  - » I used to be great in gymnastics, but I hurt my back. No more gymnastics—ever.
- loss of a first love
  - » I really liked her, but she decided she didn't like me.
- something happened—hard to explain
  - » Something else changed that's hard to talk about.

In a discussion, someone who checks the item about abuse or about something "hard to talk about" should not be prodded to talk further about it in the group if the purpose is discussion about growing up, not therapy. The facilitator, if not a counselor, can quietly ask, *after* the meeting, if the child or teen would like to talk privately with the school counselor, who can explore the issue and determine if child protective services need to be involved or if reporting and counseling have already occurred. Any facilitator, while encouraging all group members to respect privacy for the sake of trust, should explain caveats related to mandatory reporting in the initial meeting. Jean's book *Get Gifted Students Talking* provides detailed guidance for discussion group facilitators who are not professional counselors.

Being able to talk about these feelings may be life-altering for bright, sensitive kids in a high-tech era in which sustained face-to-face conversation is rare.

Small-group discussions can help children and teens find common ground with peers, but respecting privacy is essential. Group members might simply read aloud the items they checked on the list without comment, making connections with one another simply by being real. One option for discussion, also useful in individual counseling, is to have each participant choose just three checked items and describe the feelings involved and the duration of painful sadness, including if it is ongoing.

Times of transition usually involve complex emotions. Emotional struggles may last a long time. Being able to talk about these feelings may be life-altering for bright, sensitive kids in a high-tech era in which sustained face-to-face conversation is rare.

Grief in Children

When there has been a death or serious illness of someone close, or when employment or unemployment or caregiving stressors affect the family, bright children can and do grieve losses. However, they may hear adults commenting that the children, like Neeli in the vignette at the beginning of this chapter, are too young to understand what's going on. Believing that their parents can't handle additional grief, children and teens may actually try to take care of parents and siblings by not crying or talking about the changes. They may feel a loss of safety or benevolence in their world, but their asynchronous development likely leaves them emotionally unequipped to make sense of their own and others' grief. Those emotions can be scary. Young children often cannot "stay in grief" (or talk about their grief) for long at a time, appearing then to be okay. But adults should be ready to talk when the child is.

Like younger children, grieving teens may need to take a break from their grief. While adults gather to express condolences and be sad together, a teen whose parent died three days earlier might seem okay when tossing a football around outside with friends who are there to support him. Adults need to be ready for him, too, when he wants to talk.

Cultural knowledge and awareness can help support a grieving child. When Jean was conducting a study of cultural differences related to the idea of giftedness, a Native American tribal leader gave the following example of cultural disconnect. A bright seventh grader from the settlement (not a reservation) attended the public school in a nearby town. The boy's uncle checked on his well-being at school. His teacher said he'd had recent absences and was listless and uninvolved in class and in the recreation area after lunch. The uncle quietly explained that the boy's grandmother had died, and the absences were related to community grieving, typical in the culture. The uncle also expressed concern that no one had contacted the family to inquire about issues that might be associated with the absences and change in behavior. The teacher, lacking cultural awareness, simply said, "But it was only his grandmother." The grandmother had actually raised the boy.

"Figuring It Out Myself"

Bright kids, including those from stable homes, sometimes have traumatic experiences. One common example is bullying. In her study of bullying among gifted students, Jean found that even one experience of bullying in kindergarten could have long-lasting repercussions. Some interviewed students described in detail a later year of relentless bullying.

However, when asked if they told someone about being bullied, a typical response was "It was *my* problem, and I needed to figure it out." Generally kids don't understand that only someone with institutional power, or social or physical power greater than that of kids who are bullying, can stop the bullying. Otherwise, attempting to stop it might actually be dangerous. Jean has consulted in court cases involving bullying-related injury and/or suicide, including after a student stood up to a bully and was seriously harmed. When we present sessions at conferences

> The tendency for bright kids to think they need to "fix themselves" complicates their social and emotional concerns.

on bullying or childhood sexual assault, typically someone says afterward, "That was me." These adults survived, with or without professional assistance, but their faces and voices reflect disturbing memories from long ago. Parents of bullying targets often refer to their own experiences at their child's age, suggesting that anxiety increases when their child is at the age they themselves were vulnerable.

The tendency for bright kids to think they need to "fix themselves" complicates their social and emotional concerns and contributes to their despair. Jean remembers a high school sophomore who revealed in a discussion group that he was scared about "feeling so depressed." He talked about the advantage of having family financial security, but he also discreetly described a chaotic household with six children and explained that he was sleeping poorly on cushions on the floor because his dad had not finished remodeling his bedroom a year ago. He craved attention from his dad, but rarely had it. When asked if he'd talked with anyone about his sadness, he said, "Nobody likes to hang out with somebody who's depressed." So he kept smiling in the halls. The discussion group members then talked about sadness, each appearing relieved to know they weren't the only one who felt sad. Jean used this opportunity to provide the group with credible, age-appropriate psycho-educational information about depression and pertinent books for kids.

When Jean consults in school districts where children are increasingly experiencing suicidal ideation (thoughts of suicide), suicide attempts, and deaths by suicide, she often finds that bright, talented kids are among those involved. She encourages schools to create opportunities for students to develop expressive language, self-reflect, and find social and emotional common ground with intellectual peers. Through respectful face-to-face interaction, perhaps in weekly small-group discussions, they can acknowledge the stress of high expectations, embrace their cognitive strengths, and normalize the difficulty of dealing with intense, uncomfortable emotions.

Existential Depression

James Webb (2013) raised awareness of existential depression in bright children and teens. He explained that it is about disillusionment—when sensitive, idealistic kids become aware that the world is not as it should be. As these kids listen to the news; realize that big decisions in places of power are contributing to suffering; hear about cruelty, a global health crisis, weather catastrophes, and wars; worry about the health and viability of the planet; and believe they ultimately have little control in the face of these, their strong

> Many adults who are trusted by students don't know what to say—but can become a safe harbor nonetheless.

empathy and sense of fairness and justice may keep them awake at night. Witnessing aggression at school, hearing jokes and other comments that reflect racism or sexism or homophobia, or feeling constant marital tension at home can have the same effect. They may wonder about death and about imperfect relationships—and the meaning of life. When parents or guardians and teachers notice a change in energy, attitude, morale, behavior, sleep patterns, or appetite, for example, checking out these changes might lead to a conversation with a school counselor.

The average US school counselor-to-student ratio is 1:482 (NACAC and ASCA 2020). Because of the need to be proactively and reactively responsive to such a large caseload, the school counselor cannot equitably conduct *long-term* therapy with only a few students. The school counselor might therefore suggest an appointment with a counselor or psychologist in the community for serious concerns. A school counselor's training is essentially the same as that of a community mental health counselor, but with some advantages: being embedded where a student spends many hours each weekday; having opportunities for frequent brief, informal hallway or office contact with kids during and after crises; having a developmental, wellness perspective instead of focusing mostly on problem-solving; and being able to vary the duration of one-on-one meetings to match the age and attention span of the child or teen.

Adults Not Knowing What to Say

Parents and teachers may not know what to say when a child or teen clearly needs support. Jean remembers that during her many years as a high school teacher, a student from one of her classes might regularly drop by her classroom at the end of the day—usually alone. She was not a counselor at that time. In each case, she didn't know what to say—how to initiate a conversation about whatever was troubling the student. Though she tried, she knows in retrospect that she could have transformed long, awkward moments into more productive interaction. However, to her surprise, several of those memorable students contacted her years later, sometimes after a decade or more, saying something like, "Being able to come to your room helped me survive." We offer this memory here because many adults who are trusted by students don't know what to say—but can become a safe harbor nonetheless.

Those kids and others inspired Jean to change her career at midlife. The skills discussed in chapter 3, which she learned later during counselor training, would have been helpful in those after-school conversations. These skills include being gently direct by asking questions like the following—then, perhaps after some silence, simply listening:

- *What's on your mind?*

- *How would you sum up your day today?*

- *What was the worst part of your day today?*

- *How has your life been lately?*

- *I wish I knew what's going on in your head right now. Is there something you'd like to ask me?*

- *Maybe you'd just like to rest here while I make sense of my desk and get ready to catch my carpool?*

HIDING

Hiding Feelings

During the two decades Jean studied stressful life experiences and circumstances of high-ability students, she did not initially focus on hidden emotions. Yet the theme of concealing emotional pain—even extreme pain—was common, evident in the summaries below.

Gifted and LGBTQ

In a qualitative study of eighteen gifted LGBTQ young adults who reflected on their school years, 83 percent experienced depression and were suicidal at some point (Peterson and Rischar 2000). Of those, 80 percent told someone (such as a counselor or friend). But only 31 percent told a parent, and none told a teacher. The following statements suggests reasons for not talking about low morale or sexual orientation:

- "Top of my class, hyperinvolved in extracurriculars. I've suspected much of that was avoiding dealing with orientation. In structured activities, I was safe."

- About conscientiousness in academics and activities masking distress about sexual orientation, a male said, "I suppose I was such a model student and a 'joy to teach' that they didn't feel an urge to change anything—[to tell me] that I should ease up on myself."

- "My successes made me high-profile and even more reluctant to explore a possibly scandalous sexuality."

- A male explained his silence: "It's difficult to adequately articulate thoughts of sexuality at a young age."

- A female confided in her pastor, and he told her she would "go to hell."

- Another participant responded, "[The struggle over being gay] always seemed to be on my mind . . . [I was] always depressed. My emotional state was made worse by my attempts to hide [my orientation]. I made two serious attempts on my life."

- Someone who later realized he was bisexual referred to "great self-analysis, pressure, fear. I . . . was tumultuous over being just straight or gay."

High-Risk Graduates

Three of four high-risk (depression and suicidal ideation, severe underachievement, or severe family conflict) gifted high-school graduates studied in depth over four years did not tell their parents during high school about their internal chaos (Peterson 2001a). One of them, a high achiever, was distressed by family tension around his sister's poor mental health, but he did not tell anyone about this—or about his struggles related to sexual orientation. A young woman made a serious suicide attempt, and then talked with her sister and mother, but prior to that, had not talked with anyone about her growing distress over childhood memories.

Trauma Survivor

According to a talented, high-achieving female survivor of sexual trauma and domestic violence, "everything was sterling" for her at school because she did not talk about her problems—until an adult confidant there breached a promise of confidentiality (Peterson 2014). Then came isolation and thoughts of suicide. She had no support at home either. The elementary gifted-education teacher initially, and other teachers later, became crucial supporters. They recognized depression, extreme stress, and ostracism and provided safe, quiet spaces for her without knowing about the violence and incest. A local therapist also helped her survive.

Targets of Bullying

Half the targets of bullying in a national study of 456 gifted eighth-graders "never" or "not often" talked about their worries with someone (Peterson and Ray 2006b). Some students spoke of self-doubt, sadness, helplessness, fear, and feeling at fault. Their responses to bullying were intense and prolonged, especially to teasing, the kind of bullying associated with the most negative emotions.

High-Stress Female Adolescents

None of six bright female adolescents from homes that were not safe, stable, and nurturing had told anyone about their emotional upheaval until they became part of a study of young women struggling with adversity (Peterson 1998). Five were high academic achievers. They believed their successes masked their distress and that teachers were unaware of their struggles at home.

Successful Adults Who Underachieved in School

If it hadn't been for positive role models at school or in the community—and, for some, being feisty, argumentative, and angry—some participants in a study of successful former underachievers believed they would not have been successful as adults (Peterson 2001b). Most did not talk about their life with anyone. Positive change happened only after leaving home.

Bright and Troubled Early Teens

In a study of bright middle school students from low-income and distressed families, participants did not talk with school counselors about their troubles (Peterson 1997). However, most named grandparents and teachers as "nicest" and a teacher as "understands me," underscoring the importance of quiet support in the classroom and of a safe harbor outside of school.

Negative Life Events

In the study of negative life events experienced by gifted kids during the K–12 school years, the finding that stress levels increased greatly over these years suggests that those typically eligible for gifted-education programs may be affected by continual or intermittent commotion and stressors at home (Peterson, Duncan, and Canady 2009). Examples from the study follow here:

- A student didn't mention the several family deaths her parents had noted during the study, but wrote about grief over having to quit a sport she excelled at because of a chronic disease.

- Another student grieved after her sister left home for college.

- Yet another's family hosted an exchange student. The poor-fit situation disrupted her home and social life enough that she mentioned it as one of her three biggest challenges during her twelve school years. The situation was still not easy for her to talk about.

- A student's large number of absences was associated with extreme conflict between him and his parents. He had had problems with drug use. He noted that one teacher "stood by me" until "I turned things around." He indicated that the teacher was the only adult who "heard" him.

- Another student, with the highest number of completed Advanced Placement courses (twenty-one) in his class, emphatically noted the pressure he felt to keep up his reputation. He protected his public image by hiding extreme stress.

One situation from this study underscores that adults' assumptions about kids' stressors might not be accurate. When one set of parents picked up their daughter after she had completed the open-ended student questionnaire about "most challenging experiences" a few days after graduation, they asked what kinds of questions were included. They had filled out a checklist of negative events in the family annually for eleven years, and they assumed she had identified some of those troubling experiences. Instead, she said her major challenges were related to school activities and academics: "Things you thought would bother me—didn't. And some you thought didn't—did."

Two other studies are pertinent to hiding concerns from parents. In Canadian therapist Sue Jackson's clinical study of highly gifted adolescents and young adults , they hid depression because they believed revealing despair would have a toxic effect on their parents

(Jackson and Peterson 2003). In a dissertation study, Joanne Bourque Nice (2006) found that female underachievers disengaged from parents during adolescence, connecting exclusively to peers, being in nonegalitarian relationships, and believing that being sexually active represented maturity.

Hiding Distress

Positive Bias

We might assume that positive bias is preferable to negative bias in interactions with bright kids. However, when they are perceived to be amazing, they feel pressure to protect this perception, and both adults and peers may therefore assume that all is well. To many adults, high ability automatically means high achievement, and high achievement means solid mental health. But there may be a downside to appearing to be well balanced. US high school counselors may not see high achievers in their offices except for letters of recommendation, scholarship applications, schedule changes, and semi-annual check-ins. They, like other adults, may speak repeatedly of "being impressed"—with classroom achievement, success in areas of talent, or leadership. Such a positive bias may prevent counselors from recognizing, inquiring about, and attending to emotional concerns—and they may even miss evidence of high distress. Verbalizing awe of students and clients may encourage them not to show vulnerability or taint their image. They may perceive that there is too much at stake for them to admit limitations, vulnerability, doubt, guilt, or fear of failure.

> Verbalizing awe of students and clients may encourage them not to show vulnerability or taint their image.

Negative Bias

In contrast, an underachiever (or a high achiever who is arrogant, argumentative, noncompliant, or disruptive) might face negative bias. A tough or tightly woven exterior might close the door to questions about unsettling emotions, depression, or anxiety. It might even prevent discussion about adequate sleep and nutrition, about self-medication with alcohol or other drugs, and about possibilities for the future.

What Is at Stake?

High achievers in academics or talent areas may be concerned about disappointing parents, teachers, directors, coaches, and other adults. These high performers may be reluctant to show cracks in their emotional armor by openly talking about stressors and fears. Losing the support of invested adults, letting them down, or embarrassing them might be unthinkable.

Because of their wish to be in control, and their ability to maintain control, they may not risk talking about their social and emotional concerns. When there is a well-honed image in place, the thought of approaching a school counselor for nonroutine help might be frightening—for both achievers and underachievers. Teachers and coaches might ask a school counselor to talk with a student, but there is no guarantee that the student will agree to meet or to talk about concerns.

Why Don't They Tell Us?

Bright kids probably have good reasons for hiding their distress. Not all of them have emotional support at home. Not all have transportation for activities that involve competitions, performances, and after-school practices. Some students need to care for younger siblings after school hours. Sensitive kids may be keenly aware of family needs, economic constraints, or health concerns and do not want to cause commotion by complaining—or even asking to participate in activities. Because they are so capable, because family leadership is not solid, because their parents work more than one shift, or because poor parental health requires it, they may have adultlike roles at home even at a young age, contributing to adultlike worries. They believe they will need to take charge and problem-solve when scary situations arise.

Other bright kids are sensitive to their own or their family's positive public image, perhaps worrying that revealing anxiety, insomnia, sadness, self-injury, sexual orientation, or thoughts of suicide will tarnish it. Stellar athletes, musicians, and artists may be concerned about maintaining winning records, and they know that parents and mentors are invested in their success. They might also worry about how peers would react to an altered image.

Their perceptions of parents and family may be accurate, of course. If the star of the family falls apart, what happens to the family? What if the star gives the family hope for the future? Bright kids may perceive, accurately, that "nobody can understand." If something shameful has happened, they may feel they have been complicit—or should have been smart enough to avoid it. Even in the wake of sexual or other physical and emotional abuse, it's easy for them to blame themselves.

Out from Hiding

It Takes a Village—an Alert Village

When bright kids hide their biggest emotions, even their best friends may not know about their distress—and parents may also have no idea that their child or teen is suffering. Counselors, psychologists, and teachers need to be aware that parents may not see signs of distress. These professionals need to listen carefully and inquire further when parents or guardians describe what they've observed or bring up vague concerns. It is also important not to be dismissive when kids express fear, despair, hopelessness, and a bleak vision of their future—regardless of their intellect, academic and other successes, and the family's seemingly secure socioeconomic status or circumstances.

The idea that "it takes a village to raise a child" applies to school professionals and all other potential helpers. If educators sense that a child or teen is thinking about suicide, they should contact a school counselor or another school district or child services resource and make sure that person gets the message. Any layperson who senses unsettling emotions when interacting with a child or teen can also intervene and ask, without assuming the role of counselor, "You don't seem like yourself lately. Should I worry about you? (Pause.) How much should I worry? (Pause.) Have you been thinking of hurting yourself?" If the second and last answers are "yes," any of the above professionals are trained to ask further questions, call parents or guardians, and take concrete steps to ensure safety.

> "
> Making space and time available for bright kids to discuss social and emotional challenges with high-ability peers can help them normalize feelings and struggles and increase their sense of control.

Making space and time available for bright kids to discuss social and emotional challenges with high-ability peers, regardless of how they perform academically and socially, can help them normalize feelings and struggles and increase their sense of control. They discover that others have similar concerns. They develop skills in expressing emotions verbally and nonverbally, explore concerns about emotions and behavior in a safe place, and put exceptional ability into perspective. Interacting about social and emotional concerns also nudges them out of the security and isolation of an intellectual bubble that might limit their creativity and development (Vaivre-Douret 2011). Adding expressive language to their skill set and experiencing the support of like-minded peers can strengthen their foundation for current and later life.

Psychoeducation

The Peterson Proactive Developmental Attention model offers a framework for developing expressive language and social connection through talking about social and emotional challenges (Peterson and Jen 2018). Classroom, small-group, or individual psychoeducation (in this case, offering information about or exploring the process of growing up) can, for example, focus on developmental tasks: figuring out who they are and where they're going; moving in the direction of increasingly mature relationships; and becoming more and more independent while remaining healthily connected to family. Discussion might focus on whether they are feeling stuck with any of those developmental tasks and how developmental tempo varies within a general range and from one area (for example, language, psychomotor, social, emotional) to another.

In Jean's study of fourteen high-risk (severe underachievement, depression, or conflict) gifted young adults for four years after they graduated from high school, she found that accomplishing two or more (of five) developmental tasks was associated with being able to focus on, and invest in, academics (Peterson 2002). In fact, two former extreme underachievers had accomplished all four tasks and had four years of college, but three other underachievers, including two National Merit Scholars, had accomplished no developmental tasks, or just one, and had not finished college. Resolving conflict with parents and gaining autonomy preceded or converged with finding direction for some, but having many realistic career options appeared to make finding clear direction difficult for others. Autonomy, the task usually accomplished first, was associated with feeling emotionally healthy. Helping bright kids interact with intellectual peers about developmental challenges before they leave high school, regardless of achievement level, might help them feel less angst about the future, plan for it, normalize developmental challenges, and believe that change, including resolution of severe conflict with parents, is possible.

Positive Disintegration

When we are counseling bright kids, especially those experiencing extended distress in complex circumstances beyond their control, we often include psychoeducational information about Kazimierz Dabrowski's theory of positive disintegration (TPD), the sole focus of Sal Mendaglio's (2008) book and a topic addressed in several chapters of *Living with Intensity* (Daniels and Piechowski, 2009). The theory argues that struggle is essential to advanced development. When situations feel overwhelming, and the learning applied to resolve problems in the past doesn't work, "psychological disintegration" can occur—intense, unsettling, and long-lasting uncertainty and despair. One possible resolution is to return to the former, familiar level of psychological integration. But a new level of integration is also possible: advanced development reflected in autonomy, empathy, altruism, and authenticity.

The experiences of the young woman who was the subject of the fifteen-year study of development, referred to in chapter 2 and earlier in this chapter, demonstrated that struggle can be helpful, that high intelligence can help bright kids grapple with extreme distress, and that extreme self-awareness can be both a strength and a vulnerability. She experienced intense suffering, introspection, therapy, and emotional development. At age nineteen she discovered TPD when searching for helpful resources from the library. The theory helped her make sense of her long, dramatic struggle and find meaning in her emotional pain.

The intensity that characterizes bright individuals in one or more areas can exacerbate responses to troubling life events and difficult circumstances. The subject of the study mentioned above concluded that her emotional intensity pushed her forward, helping her survive, until she could apply her intellectual intensity toward understanding what she was experiencing.

Providing troubled bright kids with this kind of information, even at young ages, can help them make sense of themselves and their feelings. Circumstances such as bullying, sexual and other physical and emotional abuse, violence at home or in the community, family stressors, and serious illness or injury in self or others who are close can result in painful distress. High cognitive ability can help kids put difficulties at arm's length and make sense of them, and expressing emotions can help them heal.

Preparing for Life After High School

The transition to post–high school life involves great changes. Jean's weekly high school discussion groups for gifted students, focused on developmental challenges (see chapter 5), were an opportunity to anticipate some of those changes. In her students she witnessed the stress and high anxiety connected to choosing and applying to selective institutions, considering possible career directions, paying for college, and in some cases, worrying about academics during "senioritis" (low motivation). She knew that some of these students were the first in their families to go to college, and she guessed that some parents erroneously assumed that pertinent information would be available at school for all students. She knew that the annual evening financial aid session for students and their parents did not address social and emotional concerns. Therefore, she annually invited four to six first-year college students home on break for the Thanksgiving holiday to interact with two discussion groups during the two-hour midday lunch schedule on the day before the holiday, when school was still in session. The guests represented various kinds of institutions—small and large, private and public, far away and not so far, big-city and small-town. The intimacy of a conference room, with no more than twelve students in each group, seemed to help them, as someone usually said, feel "comfortable asking dumb questions" about college.

In the high school program for high-ability students, Jean organized all discussion groups according to grade level, because developmental concerns differed accordingly. For example, final-year students were far more focused on the transitions after high school than were students one year behind them. Thus, only discussion groups composed of seniors experienced the panel of college students. Group members wrote questions about college and university life on index cards during the preceding week, and those guided the hour-long discussions. Typical questions fell into four categories:

- **preparation:** how roommates are assigned, whether having a firm major is essential at the outset, whether roommates communicate with each other prior to arriving, what to consider when selecting a college or university

- **the first weeks:** sharing a room, what to do about a poor roommate match, finding someone to eat with, navigating a large campus without being late to classes, experiencing homesickness

- **daily life:** getting food when ill, sleeping in a noisy residence hall, avoiding weight gain, managing a credit card

- **adjustments to academics:** size of classes in large institutions, number of exams, amount of reading, access to instructors for help, self-discipline for class attendance, the impact of alcohol-related socializing on academics

By late fall, most panelists had experienced illness and some homesickness, had settled into academic and social life, and could articulate practical, social, emotional, academic, and philosophical challenges. The focus of the panel discussion was clearly about a major developmental transition, involving identity, relationships, career direction, and autonomy.

The panelists referred to being unable to bring their high school identity into the new environment, challenges related to long-distance romantic relationships, feeling less clear about career direction than when they left high school, adjusting to sharing a room, and struggling to take care of laundry. The following week, group members typically expressed gratitude for what they had learned from the panel—and for the panel's willingness to be open and vulnerable.

Important to note here is that Jean's groups at other school levels were also homogeneous in age/grade, except when gifted kids had been accelerated to a higher grade level. For those, the emphasis on social and emotional developmental usually made them a better fit with age peers, not grade-level peers. With that said, however, a radically accelerated child or teen soon entering college might benefit from the college panel, depending on expected level of autonomy and support on campus.

Counseling

Mental health professionals and educators can show interest in and validate how a child or teen experiences exceptional ability by asking questions like *What is it like to be so bright? What's the best part of it? What's the worst?* High ability affects all aspects of life. Ignoring that elephant in the room implies that it isn't important and doesn't affect relationships with peers and adults, self-expectations, sense of differentness, and being able to "turn off the mind." Based on her dissertation study, Aimee Yermish (2010) concluded that counselors and psychologists need to show curiosity about the impact of giftedness. Showing interest can prevent therapeutic rupture (harm to the essential counselor-client relationship), from which the counseling relationship may never recover.

 POINTS TO PONDER

- Bright, sensitive kids may struggle with intense emotions but keep a tight lid on them.
- They may not have a place to talk about concerns and someone to talk about them with.
- Family and teachers may not be aware of these social and emotional struggles.
- High-ability kids are often adept at hiding distress.
- Psychoeducational opportunities can inform bright kids, help them develop expressive language, and help them prepare for and cope with expected and unexpected life transitions.

Coping with Adversity

AFTER being homeless briefly, an urban family of five feels fortunate to have a two-room apartment with reliable utilities. But Dad's custodial job is now no longer available because of the COVID-19 pandemic, and he is often angry, depressed, and absent. Mom, a healthcare worker, becomes infected with the coronavirus and dies. The three kids' schools have shut down for now. L'Trel, thirteen and bright, is in charge. He is the family's best cook. Naomi, eleven, likes to clean, and E'Twon, eight, can make beds and clean the bathroom. During the summer, the kids figure out with help from a neighbor where to get food, play safely, get bus passes, get housing assistance, and find used clothes that fit. In the fall, if schools are still closed, the nearby library has computers for online learning. The kids, often home alone in recent years, have always been more self-sufficient than most kids their age. They're familiar with grocery stores and bus lines and waking up in time for school. Now, even though they are often scared about what's ahead, tired from their efforts at home, and sad about their mom and dad, they tell each other, "We'll get through this."

. . . .

Struggles, obstacles, setbacks, loss, and adversity are inevitable in life. All children and teens face them. But professionals who work with them need to consider that some are bright, resourceful kids like L'Trel and his siblings, who have more than their fair share of struggles and need support and credible validation of their resilience—but who might not provide such details unless asked.

When adults discuss the needs of bright children and teens, they often focus on educational programming and curriculum differentiation. Those are certainly important concerns. However, developing coping skills and resilience is crucial for optimal health, well-being, and social and emotional development.

Youth stress, anxiety, depression, self-medication, self-injury, and suicide have increased alarmingly in recent years. Bright children and adolescents may be at least as vulnerable as their age peers in the general population (if not more so) to these experiences and behaviors, according to the study mentioned at the outset of chapter 9. Yet, with highly capable kids, it's easy to assume otherwise.

WHAT IS RESILIENCE AND WHEN DOES IT FALL SHORT?

Resilience is the capacity to bounce back—to rise above difficult circumstances and recover from setbacks. Dan Siegel and Tina Bryson (2018) define resilience as being resourceful in responding to life's challenges and dealing with them with strength and clarity. According to pediatrician Kenneth Ginsburg (2015), a nationally recognized expert on resilience, resilient people tend to see obstacles as opportunities and seek solutions. They push through challenges and learn from their mistakes. As a result, they become increasingly more confident in their ability to deal with adversity and challenge. Children and teens reach their resilience limits when external demands exceed their internal coping abilities.

Unfortunately, bright kids commonly reach their limits because of stress, social challenges, and pressure at school, but other struggles may include family conflict, financial and housing problems, and grief and loss. Helping these kids increase their internal ability to cope and respond to their external stressors is important. Some signs that children's coping skills are maxed out are these:

- physical symptoms such as headaches, stomachaches, dizziness, feeling light-headed
- fatigue
- lack of interest in school and activities
- poor academic performance
- sadness
- irritability and anger
- substance abuse as self-medication
- self-harm—cutting, burning, rubbing skin until it bleeds, disordered eating

Perfectionism (see chapter 8) often has a role in emotional burnout and breakdown of coping and resilience in bright children. Perfectionistic characteristics we have seen clinically as a source of constant tension and stress are these:

- self-loathing
- never feeling good enough
- never producing anything good enough
- no outside-the-box thinking
- no creativity
- lack of risk-taking or trying something new
- inability to receive constructive feedback
- lack of joy when experiencing success

In the retrospective study of negative events in the lives of gifted kids mentioned earlier, stress levels increased with each successive school level (Peterson, Duncan, and Canady 2009). On a scale from 1 to 10, the average stress level in elementary school was 2.7, in middle school 5.8, and in high school 6.8. The most common stress level was 1 in elementary, 5 in middle, and 8 in high school. It is noteworthy that some middle and high school students experienced stress at level 10.

BUILDING RESILIENCE

In this chapter, we focus on building resilience in the midst of stressful challenges. One key factor appears consistently in studies of resilient people: connection to one person who believes in them and supports them unconditionally. Anyone reading this book can be that person for a bright child or teen—parent or guardian, grandparent, aunt, uncle, teacher, coach, employer, or mentor, for example. *Unconditional* support is especially important because many bright kids, whether performing well or not, believe they are worthy only when they are doing something, winning something, impressing someone, or meeting high expectations. When caring adults focus their attention on wellness regardless of performance, the whole child can be embraced.

> One key factor appears consistently in studies of resilient people: connection to one person who believes in them and supports them unconditionally.

Building resilience involves helping a child stretch and grow. Children and teens typically rise (or fall) to the expectations set for them. When expectations are too high for current abilities and development, kids are likely to feel defeated and give up. If expectations are too low, kids miss opportunities to persevere and push themselves. An effective strategy is to set expectations just beyond reach. When they stretch a little, kids learn to tolerate setbacks in the process of learning. They not only learn a new skill or enhance a current skill, but also experience the feeling of trying something difficult, working at it, and eventually succeeding. They learn that success comes from ability plus effort, not just from naturally endowed ability.

Experiencing adversity is an important component of building resilience. "Helicopter parenting," in which parents remove obstacles in their children's paths and anxiously help them avoid discomfort and pain, *prevents* a child from building resilience. Even after their kids leave home for further education, these parents may be in frequent contact with university professionals, trying to communicate with professors when test scores or papers aren't satisfactory (Lythcott-Haimes 2015). In order to foster resilience, adults need to encourage age-appropriate autonomy and not focus on protecting kids from all adversity and disappointment. Kids need to have opportunities to dig deep and succeed, as well as work hard and fail. Through these experiences, kids learn that they can find their way through the fog, that they have personal strengths to rely on, that plans don't always work out, and that life goes on regardless. These realizations will likely help them in special relationships, parenting, and employment in the future.

We have generally noticed the following characteristics in resilient individuals in our clinical work:

- being able to engage others with solid social skills
- being able to communicate feelings to others
- being able to tolerate distress
- finding substitute caregivers (for example, a relative, a friend's parent, a trusted neighbor, or a church, synagogue, or mosque youth leader) when needed; having positive role models outside of the home
- having a few good relationships, relationships that involve trust, and a good support network
- having initiative; being able to function independently
- being flexible and adaptable
- having self-confidence and clarity when facing complex challenges
- having good impulse control from within, rather than from an external source
- being motivated to achieve; performing well in school
- having intelligence, special talents, insight

Some of the above, and additional factors of resilience as well, are included in the following summaries of six bright, at-risk young women Jean studied in her first years as a researcher (Peterson 1998). In stark contrast to children and teens with hovering parents, these resilient women all survived danger and distress mostly independently. Their strengths offer hope that even in dire circumstances, bright, sensitive students can gain perspective, adapt, and survive.

Tiffany:

- was a proactive problem-solver in getting what she needed at school
- did not blame herself for family problems and was clear about who was responsible for them
- had a crucial confidant in her sister

Brittany:

- could articulate her strengths
- adapted by developing cooking skills and not wilting when her father berated her

- had a relative with a place for her to retreat to
- listened to and internalized rare compliments from teachers
- used her anger, drive, impatience, and destructive impulses to, as she said, "keep life interesting"

Angela:

- through intelligence, problem-solving, and trusting a counselor, gained insight into her complex family situation and conquered her anxieties
- had crucial unconditional support from a relative and from mentors at school
- was nurtured early in life

Christie:

- in college, found friendships, academics that challenged her, and greater ease with peers
- proactively sought help at a critical time when she needed to leave high school for a while
- moved forward to a large university, where she could both lose and find herself
- had a confidant in her mother and had supportive friends

Mary:

- learned problem-solving through caring for younger siblings in a low-structure home
- was adaptable, had supportive friends, and was close to her mother
- recognized and embraced her own intelligence and competence
- maintained distance from negative influences in her community
- used counseling to replace poor boundaries with healthy autonomy

Megan:

- struggled alone when her parents responded inappropriately to her being traumatized as a child, but gradually learned to trust supportive adults outside the home
- single-mindedly pursued clear goals
- had a sibling confidant and relatives to be comfortable with
- in spite of anxiety and self-harm, had a positive view of herself and her talents

The 7 Crucial Cs

Ginsburg's (2015) 7 Crucial Cs offer guidance for helping kids build resilience:

1. **Competence:** Adults can help children consider options wisely and safely. Adults can teach skills that help kids develop competence for handling situations effectively.

2. **Confidence:** Children's confidence comes from knowing and trusting their capabilities and strengths. Gaining confidence through successes gives them courage to test whether they can master more challenging tasks.

3. **Connection:** Children positively connected to family, friends, school, and community are likely to have a sense of security, strong values, and little likelihood of seeking destructive behaviors. Children who are well connected to their school are more likely to thrive educationally, emotionally, and socially. If they view school as a safe place with adults who care about their well-being, children are more likely to find learning pleasurable and rewarding.

4. **Character:** When people have well-grounded values, they can rely on these during crises, contributing to resilience. Dan recalls his mid-twenties, when he saw a bumper sticker that said, "If you don't stand for something, you stand for nothing." After a brief panic about not knowing what he stood for, he was able to identify strong values that helped him navigate a difficult time of life.

5. **Contribution:** Having opportunities to contribute to school, community, church, synagogue, or mosque, and guidance about how to do that, can help kids develop a sense of purpose, empathy for others, and the ability to focus on others. Making a difference in the life of another can serve as an antidote to feeling isolated, detached, overwhelmed, and depressed. (Chapter 9 includes information about existential depression.) Contribution gives kids a sense that they matter and that the world is better because they are in it. When they help others, they realize that others can help them as well.

6. **Coping:** Children who can cope with and manage stress are prepared for life's challenges. With a range of positive coping strategies practiced and available (such as talking with someone, taking a walk, exercising, and yoga), they are less likely to engage in high-risk behaviors.

7. **Control:** Believing they have some control over their universe rather than being at its mercy helps children and teens do what is necessary to bounce back from adversity. This belief is related to the idea of locus of control. People with an internal locus of control believe they are responsible for results, whereas people with an external locus of control believe what happens is beyond their control.

Each of the 7 Cs builds on the preceding C. According to Ginsburg, when children feel *competent*, they begin to feel *confident* about their abilities. When they feel confident, they are more comfortable connecting with others. Through *connection*, they learn what is important to themselves and others, helping them develop *character*. With character, they realize the importance of *contributing* to their community, experience a sense of purpose, and feel supported. This awareness helps them *cope* with social and emotional challenges and access resources for support. Finally, with these coping skills, they feel *control* over what they can do when life is difficult or when their plans don't work out.

The vignette about the resilience of L'Trel and his siblings reflects the 7 Cs in practical terms. Necessity required *competence*, and the kids developed *confidence* in their domestic skills as their competence increased. Their family had more than superficial *connection* to neighbors. They developed *character* through knowing how crucial their *contributions* were at home, and as they continued to cope with their difficult circumstances, they felt some *control*. Their parents had channeled their kids' abilities and emotions into responsible, cooperative behavior at home. But having adult roles, including being the "bottom line" in crises, can create anxiety. Being able to talk with a school counselor, grandparent, or neighbor can help kids with heavy responsibilities de-stress and survive. In general, when parents or other influential adults can credibly call attention to any of the Cs in conversation, after having had time to observe and identify them, a child or teen may be able to self-affirm them in the future when stressed.

> Five bright, resilient boys in extreme circumstances beat the odds. Each had at least one teacher who went far beyond a typical level of investment of energy and time to support them.

The 7 Cs are also reflected in Thomas Hébert's book *Talented Young Men Overcoming Tough Times: An Exploration of Resilience* (2018). The book is composed of stories of five bright, resilient boys in extreme circumstances who beat the odds. Each had at least one teacher who went far beyond a typical level of investment of energy and time to support them. Success during special opportunities for kids with high potential led to friendships that were important for developing an identity as a talented boy. Perseverance, focusing on the future, practical intelligence, and outlets for talent development, social action, and leadership were additional themes.

Real Tiger or Paper Tiger?

With his youngest clients, Dan often uses a simple yet powerful tool inspired by Kenneth Ginsburg (2015) to help them deal with adversity. The first step is teaching them how a small part of the brain called the amygdala reacts like a fire alarm in frightening situations. Young bright kids like the word *amygdala*—and might be able to tell that part of their brain to calm down when they are scared. When they have learned about the fight-or-flight response, they can understand what is happening to them. They learn that their brain responds to fear in this way to keep them safe from tigers (and other dangers faced by their prehistoric ancestors). Dan teaches children to ask themselves, when they begin to feel fear, "Is there a real tiger or a paper tiger trying to eat me?" The touch of humor in this question is helpful, especially when it's asked *before* a full-fledged fight-or-flight response. When bright children realize that the thing they are afraid of is not life-threatening, or is not as bad as they thought, or is indeed terrible, they can deactivate their emotional brain, reactivate their thinking brain, and use their coping and problem-solving skills. That is, even in wretched circumstances, they can access the strengths and resilience they have developed. They learn to ask themselves questions like *Does my reaction fit the situation? Will I feel this way tomorrow, next week, next month, or next year?* Chapter 7 includes additional detail about brain responses.

The ABCs of Resilience

In their book *The Resilience Factor* (2002), Karen Reivich and Andrew Shatté present the ABCs of resilience. They explain that in order to respond to *adversity* (A) effectively, people must recognize their *beliefs* (B) and consider the *consequences* (C) of their behavior during a challenging moment. These components are similar to those in cognitive approaches to managing anxiety (see chapter 7). When adults are guiding kids, the ABCs look like this:

- **Challenge beliefs.** Teach kids to notice their thinking and generate alternatives to those thoughts. Teach them to look for evidence that their thinking is accurate (for example, asking, "Do I really *never* have anyone to talk to at recess?").

- **Put beliefs into perspective.** Help kids generate worst-case beliefs, then healthier, less catastrophic counterbeliefs, and then make a plan for dealing with the anxiety-producing situation: For example, "I am going to fail my math test" can be changed to "My math tests are hard, but I always seem to do pretty well (or well enough)." Then help them think about how they can approach taking the test (for example, "I am going to study like I usually do and then wake up early and go over my notes").

- **Develop real-time resilience.** Help kids develop a plan for managing responses to unsettling situations. For example, a bright child who is nervous about not having someone to talk to at lunch might manage worrisome thoughts by thinking, "I am worried I won't have someone to talk to at lunch, but I have other options planned if it happens." The plan might be to go to the library, visit a teacher, or look for a new person from class to talk with.

Learning to manage challenging day-to-day situations helps them develop resilience for whatever they face throughout life—personal tragedy, disaster, threats to health and safety, or difficult relationships, for example.

Grit

Angela Lee Duckworth's 2013 TED Talk on grit went viral, and she later wrote an informative book on the topic, *Grit: The Power and Passion of Perseverance*. Duckworth explained that, in her experience as a teacher and later as a psychologist, she found that kids who showed grit (and did not necessarily have high capability) had better outcomes than kids who were smart and did not show grit. Imagine what is possible for a child who is smart *and* has grit.

So what is grit, and how can we get it? Grit is working hard, being diligent, and having perseverance. Duckworth says that commitment to hard work and practice may predict success in life better than intelligence can. Further, people who learn to overcome adversity are thought to have lifelong grit—in other words, resilience.

When Dan teaches kids about grit, he shares the following maxims, which have uncertain origins: *Opportunity is missed by most people because it is dressed in overalls and looks like work* and *The harder I work, the luckier I seem to get*. These sayings emphasize showing up, working hard, and persevering. It is important for bright kids to understand that how hard they work—not just showing up and using their natural abilities—probably determines whether they reach their goals.

Mindset

The concept of mindset was introduced by Carol Dweck in her seminal 2006 book, *Mindset: The New Psychology of Success*. Her decades of research led to her theory of two types of mindset: a fixed mindset and a growth mindset. People with a fixed mindset are focused on outcomes—prizes, grades, scores, achievement. People with a growth mindset are more interested in process than outcome, more interested in learning than grades. With a fixed mindset, people believe that they are as smart as they will ever be, and that being smart means being able to do well without effort. With a growth mindset, people are focused on learning and view their brain as a muscle that becomes stronger with exercise (Dweck 2016).

> It is important for bright kids to understand that how hard they work—not just showing up and using their natural abilities—probably determines whether they reach their goals.

Unfortunately, many caring parents and teachers inadvertently promote a fixed mindset with statements like, *Another 100 percent! You're so smart!* or *You're so good at that!* Although these are common, reasonable statements, they do not take into account that bright kids often don't have to exert themselves to do well in school. Yet effort will likely be necessary for success throughout their education and adulthood. Ideally, classroom teachers differentiate curriculum so that the brightest students must invest time and effort, and special programs include stimulating options that go beyond the usual curriculum and stretch their minds. Recognizing the power of effort may lead to resilience in the face of obstacles—large or small, personal or professional, at home or in school, in the family or in relationships, or with responsibilities at work.

Resilience, grit, and a growth mindset are associated with health and well-being. Adults can help bright children build a growth mindset by focusing on the following:

- effort as important to outcome

- persistence as important to mastery

- mistakes as part of growth

- process as valuable as outcome

- problem-solving

- engaging them in both independent and collaborative learning

Technology and Screens

We could not have a chapter about resilience without at least mentioning screens. We are living within a human experiment involving technology that affects everyone, especially children and teens. In fact, the pandemic era has diminished face-to-face interaction, expanded online communication, and made less brick-and-mortar contact and more online learning and talent development "normal." It is difficult to imagine how these changes, relatively sudden and deeper than the previous gradual drift into tech-driven life, will affect social skills, trust in relationships, what is learned, how we think, and how resilient we will be in the near and distant future.

The upside of living so much online is that more student-to-student and school-to-school collaboration is possible. Online classes might actually become more interactive than in-person classes, depending on the creativity of teachers. Nonschool online interaction can level the social playing field in positive ways. Shy kids, those living in rural areas or small towns, and kids who are ostracized at school may find mind-mates and interest groups online, moving them forward socially.

However, for kids of any age, the possible negatives of spending a great amount of time online include seeing disturbing video images, naively sharing personal information and trusting personal profiles, and being vulnerable to predators. Cyberbullying, no longer a new phenomenon, can be a threat anywhere and at any time, not just at school. The anonymity that is possible online allows socially aggressive students to feel invisible, powerful, unlikely to be punished, and increasingly uninhibited and unconcerned about judgment. Online communication also allows targets of traditional or cyberbullying to retaliate, using phone or laptop as a weapon. When done online, the jockeying for social position that characterizes some traditional bullying can be particularly cruel and vicious. The ripple effects of any of the above, which can certainly test resilience, can be long-lasting and even tragic.

Any of the negatives above can affect a child's or teen's development and well-being profoundly—especially for those with heightened sensitivity and intense responses to stimuli. Excessive or inappropriate screen time can have the following impacts on children and adolescents:

- preoccupation with screens, even when they are not available

- distractibility, difficulty focusing on tasks

- staying up late and/or waking up early to maximize screen time

- irritability

- reactivity

- anxiety

- fatigue

- depression

When parents, grandparents, guardians, educators, or other invested adults see any of the above, it is important and wise to look further into screen use and content, and if needed, make a screen use plan.

Stress Reduction

With resilience in mind, and because stress is inevitable (and some kinds potentially beneficial), talking about stress at arm's length, objectively, is likely to help anyone understand it and figure out ways to appreciate it or address it. Appealing to bright kids' cognitive strengths, adults can help them identify and rank negative stressors according to the emotional and physiological impact of each. Jean's *Get Gifted Students Talking* (2020) includes background information and three guided discussions for sorting out stress and evaluating coping ability. Identifying the context for each stressor (for example, using a phone during the night, spending too much time on social media, procrastinating with homework, socializing dangerously) might reveal that one or more is avoidable, that specific strategies for coping with each might tamp down the effects, or that simply leaving some activities and concerns behind can have major benefits. In general, maintaining good health through exercise, paying attention to nutrition, and getting adequate sleep are positive ways to cope. Talking with trusted friends and relatives, making lists, laughing, crying, or regularly setting aside time for writing, yoga, or daily meditation can also help release tension. Being intentional and purposeful with self-care, not just impulsive and erratic, is ideal. All of these actions are likely to increase a sense of confidence and control, two ingredients of resilience.

> Maintaining good health through exercise, paying attention to nutrition, and getting adequate sleep are positive ways to cope.

An Activity

Jean developed an "I Am Resilient" checklist, based on research findings in various fields, to use in individual and group counseling or for small-group discussion with adolescents. After hearing a definition of *resilience*, participants simply check the statements that are true for them. No particular total number of checked items reflects solid resilience. Instead, the value is in each participant, in turn, reading aloud *all* their checked sentences at one time, with the group listening attentively. An alternate use of the activity is for participants to rate each item on a scale of 1 to 10 (10 being "very") to reflect how true each item is for them. Participants can then share their responses by going around the group for each item, read by the leader, with each person reporting a personal rating. After all in a group have responded, the leader can invite discussion about how the items on the list might reflect or contribute to resilience. To conclude, the group (or an individual) can explain what provoked thought during the activity, how they felt when reading their list, if they were surprised by their (or others') responses, and when in their life they have been resilient. Kids from chaotic, tenuous, dangerous, or otherwise insecure homes or neighborhoods usually appreciate learning about resilience and that a strong-sounding word like *resilient* describes them.

I AM RESILIENT

☐ 1. I have a person available who cares a lot about me.

☐ 2. Difficult situations usually don't overwhelm me.

☐ 3. I have a good mind that helps me survive difficult situations.

☐ 4. I am optimistic about my future.

☐ 5. I know when and how to ask for help.

☐ 6. I have good personal boundaries. I am not easily sucked into others' strong emotions. I stay clearheaded when people around me are dramatically emotional.

☐ 7. I don't believe I'm to blame for my family's difficulties.

☐ 8. I know who I am, and that gives me strength.

☐ 9. I am flexible and adaptable. I can handle changes without getting upset.

☐ 10. I am strong emotionally. I'm not afraid to feel emotions, and I don't panic or "fall apart" when I'm disappointed, hurt, scared, or stressed.

☐ 11. I have good coping skills. I know how to problem-solve in bad situations.

☐ 12. I usually bounce back after difficult experiences.

☐ 13. I can name five personal strengths I can rely on.

☐ 14. I can name five things I do well.

☐ 15. I can talk about feelings comfortably.

Final Considerations

Helping bright children and teens develop resilience can inoculate them against long-term negative effects of adversity and struggle. To help bright children grow and develop, consider these perspectives:

- Sometimes the best action to help children is to get out of their way—so they can learn how to make decisions, develop plans, and persevere in areas of interest.

- Adults attentively listening to children and teens is more important than what the adults say.

- Seeing how adults manage life challenges successfully can help children and teens do the same.

POINTS TO PONDER

To prepare bright kids for navigating crises, consider these guidelines:

- Help them assess the immediacy and credibility of a threat.
- Help them develop strategies to address problems.
- Help them develop strategies to diminish the effects of stress.
- Model how to handle stress and adversity.
- Commit to supporting them unconditionally—regardless of their behavior, their performance in the classroom or in an area of talent, or their circumstances.

Diagnosing and Misdiagnosing

TEACHERS are aware that shy, musically talented Phan, age eleven, has always been at the 99th percentile on standardized tests. But at the sixth-grade team meeting, one teacher notes with a judgmental tone that Phan seems "one step behind" socially. His grandparents were among the Vietnamese refugees arriving in the United States in the early 1980s. They had a sponsor, found work, valued education, and passed their strong work ethic on to their children and grandchildren. Phan's teachers are puzzled by his uneven classroom performance, and he himself is frustrated and unnerved about these gaps. Illustrations in textbooks distract him, and he daydreams and loses focus easily. He forgets to study the Greek gods, fails a test, and sleeps poorly for a week. He is a perfectionistic pianist at home, easily absorbed in the music, but when he's asked to accompany the choir at school, he feels tense and unconnected to the piano and has difficulty following the director. When he and classmates run around the edges of the school campus for physical education, he wonders why everyone else cuts corners when the sidewalk turns, not staying on the sidewalk. He wants to be good, to be moral. At a summer camp, when a counselor speaks to Phan and his cabin mates about a missing camera, Phan's distracted eyes and vague smile are interpreted as guilt. The counselor meets with him, and Phan explains that he was lost in thought—but he is horrified that someone thought he stole something. It isn't until late in high school that a teacher, after a workshop on autism, refers Phan to the school psychologist for an evaluation for Asperger's disorder. She knows it is now referred to as "high-functioning autism."

. . . .

Just as few educators are trained to teach bright children, few family practitioners, pediatricians, psychiatrists, psychologists, and psychotherapists are trained in the social and emotional characteristics and development of bright kids. This lack of training and awareness can lead to misdiagnoses, "a mismatch between the gifted child's actual learning and health needs and the perception of those needs by others" (Webb et al. 2016). This mismatch results in either giving a child a mental health or learning disorder diagnosis when their behaviors or concerns are better explained by giftedness (misdiagnosis), or overlooking a health disorder or learning need (missed diagnosis) because an evaluator assumes the differentness of giftedness explains the mental health and/or behavioral concerns. Misdiagnosis can result in inappropriate interventions, including when no intervention is warranted, and a missed diagnosis can lead to no treatment or ineffective treatment. With both missed diagnosis and misdiagnosis, not validating the presence and complexity of giftedness, and instead viewing behaviors reflecting giftedness as pathology only, can negatively affect identity development and diminish self-confidence.

INCREASED MENTAL HEALTH DIAGNOSES

In addition to the lack of training among medical and mental health professionals, the dramatic increase in number of available mental health diagnoses over the past few decades has played a role in misdiagnosis in the general population and of bright children in particular. The first edition of the *Diagnostic and Statistical Manual of Mental Disorders* (DSM) in 1952 had 106 diagnostic categories. Seventy years later, the DSM-5 has 539 diagnostic categories. All 539 describe pathology, a constellation of behaviors that cause significant impairment in one or more aspects of life.

With so many diagnostic categories to describe human behavior and a focus on pathology (what is wrong with someone), professionals are increasingly diagnosing the behavior of more children and adolescents as pathology. In general, at any given time, approximately 11 to 20 percent of children in the United States have a behavioral or emotional disorder as defined in the DSM-5 (Weitzman and Wegner 2015). ADHD diagnoses in children and adolescents in the United States increased 66 percent from 2000 to 2010, and psychostimulant medications were used in approximately 90 percent of cases (Garfield et al. 2012). According to a Centers for Disease Control and Prevention national parent survey, 9.4 percent of US children had been diagnosed at some time with ADHD (CDC 2019). As of 2017, one in sixty-eight children in the United States had received a diagnosis of autism spectrum disorder, according to the National Center for Complementary and Integrative Health (NCCIH 2017).

CHARACTERISTICS THAT CAN BE MISINTERPRETED AND MISUNDERSTOOD

As discussed in chapter 2, bright individuals may exhibit intensities and sensitivities in various areas, often referred to as overexcitabilities (Daniels and Piechowski 2009).

- People with *psychomotor* overexcitability may exhibit constant movement, strong drive, energy, and extended periods of activity.

- Those with *intellectual* overexcitability show insatiable curiosity and voracious appetite and capacity for intellectual effort and stimulation.

- People with *sensual* overexcitability have heightened experiences of seeing, smelling, tasting, touching, and hearing, which may include both an appreciation for aesthetics and negative reactions to sensory stimuli.

- *Imaginationally* overexcitable individuals have an active imaginary and fantasy life that is often vividly real to them.

- Those with *emotional* overexcitability have capacity for emotional depth and empathy and feel their own and others' emotions intensely.

· ·

ANDREW is ten years old and in fifth grade. He absorbs information like a sponge. His parents don't understand how he knows what he knows. He appears to have a photographic memory, is several years advanced in math, and expresses himself in writing beyond his years, though his handwriting is difficult to read. Andrew has an adult vocabulary and sounds like a professor when he speaks. He has obsessive interests that range from astrophysics to computer coding, and even in preschool he knew names and details about planets, stars, cars, and all countries, for example. He demands that all tags be cut out of his clothes, wears only the same two shirts day after day, and eats a limited number of foods.

At school, he talks and asks questions constantly, frustrating his teacher. His body is restless, and he distracts and annoys other students with his pencil tapping. He is often told to pay attention when he is spotted reading a book under his desk or staring out the window. Yet despite his apparent inattention, he always knows the answer when asked about the content at hand.

Andrew has trouble making and keeping friends. He often misses social cues. He becomes fearful at bedtime when it is dark and quiet, as he finds himself being unable to think about anything other than death and what happens when someone is dying. He describes fearing this unknown and not wanting to leave his family or to be left by his family. Andrew also has intense periods of sadness and hopelessness, when he needs to be comforted by his mother. He cannot describe what he is sad about or why he feels this way. These episodes generally last for about two hours, and he is usually fine later that day or the day after.

· ·

Andrew's behaviors or symptoms of interest to an evaluator are as follows:

- obsessive interests
- poor handwriting
- aversion to clothing tags
- limited food preferences
- constant talking
- restlessness
- distracting others
- missing social cues
- fearfulness
- sadness
- hopelessness

Andrew has symptoms of ADHD (always talking, restless, and distracting others), autism spectrum disorder or ASD (obsessive interests, professorial speech, missing social cues), sensory processing disorder (aversion to tags, limited range of foods and interests), dysgraphia (poor handwriting), anxiety (fearfulness), and depression (sadness and hopelessness). He also appears to have multiple overexcitabilities, such as psychomotor (constant talking, restlessness), intellectual (asking questions, obsessive interests, and advanced knowledge), sensual (dislike of tags and eating a limited number of foods), and emotional (fearfulness and sadness). Are Andrew's symptoms explained by some or all of the diagnoses mentioned above? Are Andrew's behaviors due to his advanced intellectual capacity and overexcitabilities?

COMMON MISDIAGNOSES IN BRIGHT KIDS

The disorders most commonly misdiagnosed or missed in bright individuals are ADHD and ASD (Gates 2009; Rimm, 2011; Webb et al. 2016). These conditions are often misdiagnosed when assessors do not take into account bright children's school curricula (which may be redundant, repetitive, and below their current knowledge and capabilities) nor do they determine whether symptoms cause significant impairment in one or more areas of a child's life, warranting diagnosis. Being bored and unstimulated often leads to distraction, inattention, and disengagement, which mimic symptoms associated with ADHD. Further, behavior that may seem quirky or different must cause significant impairment to warrant a clinical diagnosis.

In addition to ADHD and ASD, other common categories of misdiagnoses in bright kids are these (Webb et al. 2016):

- **anger disorders:** oppositional defiant disorder (ODD), conduct disorder, intermittent explosive disorder (IED), impulse control disorders, narcissistic personality disorder

- **anxiety disorders:** obsessive-compulsive disorder (OCD), obsessive-compulsive personality disorder (OCPD), social (pragmatic) communication disorder, social anxiety disorder

- **mood disorders:** bipolar disorder, cyclothymic disorder, depressive disorder, disruptive mood dysregulation disorder (DMDD)

- **learning and neurodevelopmental disorders:** dysgraphia, speech delay, dyslexia, sensory-processing disorder, central auditory processing disorder (CAPD)

Specific behaviors that may be misassessed and misdiagnosed are daydreaming, high activity level, perfectionism, power struggles, arguing, stubbornness, refusing to do homework, being self-absorbed and showing off knowledge, social difficulties, narrow interests, anxiety, explosive anger, and sleeping little. However, symptoms of disorders do not necessarily mean that a diagnosis is warranted. Sometimes offering a more challenging curriculum, altering teaching approaches, or intentionally and regularly validating creative thinkers can resolve problems.

Bright children are at risk for being misdiagnosed with an anger diagnosis because of their tendency to be confident in their knowledge and abilities, assert themselves, correct others, question authority, be emotionally reactive, and be unable to tolerate injustice.

> Symptoms of disorders do not necessarily mean that a diagnosis is warranted. Sometimes offering a more challenging curriculum, altering teaching approaches, or intentionally and regularly validating creative thinkers can resolve problems.

Perfectionistic tendencies, obsessive rituals, facial and other body tics, shyness and introversion, and social anxiety may be misdiagnosed as OCD or ASD. Intensities and sensitivities due to overexcitabilities may be misdiagnosed as mood disorders such as bipolar disorder and cyclothymic disorder, which are associated with mood cycling (a pattern of repeated, extreme changes) and the newer diagnosis of disruptive mood dysregulation disorder (DMDD). On the other hand, learning and neurodevelopmental disorders may be *missed* because of a bright child's compensatory skills and grade-level classroom performance, which are noted in the discussion about twice-exceptionality in chapter 6.

Some professionals in the field of gifted education say, usually tongue-in-cheek, that giftedness should be a diagnosis or diagnostic category. Others in the field find the notion of "pathologizing" giftedness abhorrent. Regardless, resistance to the idea of diagnosis reflects the notion that characteristics associated with high ability often explain the behavior of bright children and teens. That is, their behavior may be aberrant, but it does not represent pathology.

REASONS FOR REFERRAL

Misdiagnosis can occur when a child is referred to a medical, mental health, or educational professional because of an emotional or behavioral concern. In the following table, on the left are common reasons bright children and adolescents are referred, and on the right are associated gifted characteristics (Amend and Peters 2012).

As the table shows, when pathology is the default perspective, looking through a giftedness lens often provides an alternative explanation for behavior. This is not to say that the behaviors are not problematic. But the lens through which adults view the problem determines how they approach it. For example, if a problem is seen as due to high ability, the intervention might involve academic and environmental differentiation. If a problem is seen as warranting a mental, emotional, or behavioral diagnosis, the intervention may involve counseling and medication.

Reasons for Referral	Associated Gifted Characteristics
boredom with routine tasks or failure to finish classroom work or homework	rapid pace of learning and mastery; repetition considered unnecessary
attention problems; seeming not to be focused on the classroom	poor fit with unchallenging or underchallenging curriculum
reluctance to move to a new topic of discussion	thirst for deeper meaning and understanding
self-criticism and impatience with failure	perfectionism; unwillingness to take risks
frequent, strong disagreements with parents, teachers, or peers	idealism; keen disappointment; memory, understanding, and other intellectual strengths
nonconformity; refusal to accept authority	strong-willed behavior; tendency to engage in unproductive power struggles
attempts to dominate others	bossy, misguided attempts at leadership
inappropriate or poorly timed joking or punning	creativity and unusual sense of humor without tact, judgment, or timing
emotional sensitivity, overreacting, or low frustration tolerance (easily upset over minor incidents)	overexcitabilities
messy homework; lack of interest in details	visual-spatial, nonlinear learning style
academic underachievement	disengagement with curriculum that is not meaningful or doesn't meet needs

FACTORS TO CONSIDER WHEN DIAGNOSING

Accurate diagnosis serves several purposes. It helps qualified professionals communicate complex information efficiently, it guides intervention and treatment, it helps the struggling child and family make sense of symptoms, and it allows access to services through healthcare and schools (Webb et al. 2016). Reducing misunderstanding and misdiagnosis requires a thoughtful approach to understanding the context, frequency, and severity of difficulties; determining whether the challenges persist across settings; and exploring whether the challenges diminish with environmental modifications. Multiple explanations are possible for each behavior or clinical trait.

When licensed mental health and medical professionals are considering whether a child meets criteria for a clinical diagnosis, they should ask the following questions to increase the accuracy of diagnoses and reduce misdiagnoses (Amend and Peters 2012; Peters 2016; Webb et al. 2016):

- **Does the child's developmental history indicate early milestones or precocious development?** A developmental history provides information about whether an infant or toddler was highly observant, spoke early, had an advanced vocabulary, counted to one hundred at an early age and was solving arithmetic problems precociously, was inquisitive, and/or was highly creative.

When pathology is the default perspective, looking through a giftedness lens often provides an alternative explanation for behavior.

- **Are the child's behavior patterns typical for gifted children?** Does the child relate well with older children, adults, and elders? Does the child enjoy pursuing a topic in depth and make insightful observations about it? On the first day of school, does the child already know the content being taught in that grade?

- **Are the child's problem behaviors found only in certain situations or contexts, rather than across most situations?** Does the child have difficulty only in the classroom or only on the playground? Does the child have difficulty only with same-age peers? Does the child have difficulty only with authority figures who tend to demand compliance without questioning? Does the child have strong emotional reactions only with situations that involve fairness and justice issues?

- **Do the problem behaviors diminish when the child is with other gifted people or in intellectually supportive settings?** Do the child's social issues diminish in the company of like-minded children? Is the child able to sustain attention in an intellectually engaging class or activity? Does the child's depressed mood or anxiety decrease when with others who think as the child does and have similar interests?

- **Can the child's problem behaviors be explained as stemming from a highly able or creative person being in a poor-fit or threatening situation?** Do emotional meltdowns and aggression diminish when the child is removed from peers who are teasing or bullying? Do oppositional responses decrease when teachers, coaches, and mentors allow the child to question them and when they answer the child's questions respectfully and thoughtfully?

- **Do the child's behaviors cause impairment in personal or social functioning, or are they simply quirks or idiosyncrasies that cause little actual impairment or discomfort?** Do the child's inattention and lack of focus affect learning and productivity? Do the child's strong reactions to injustice on the playground negatively affect friendships? Does the child's need to be in charge and in control affect relationships? Do the rituals or routines disrupt the child's daily life?

Asking these questions can help adults determine whether it's a child's exceptional ability or a diagnosable impairment that is contributing to the emotions and behaviors that are of concern. In the following table are some issues that clinical professionals commonly see, with explanations according to the lens used during evaluation (Peters 2016).

CLINICAL TRAITS VIEWED THROUGH DIFFERENT LENSES

Clinical Trait	The Gifted Lens	Potential Diagnoses
High activity level	Passionate learner; kinesthetic learner	Possibly ADHD
Frequent worrying	Idealism; grappling with moral, ethical, philosophical, and spiritual issues	Possibly anxiety disorder; depression
High sensitivity to loud noise, clothing tags, fluorescent lights	Overexcitabilities	Possibly sensory processing disorder; CAPD
Difficulty relating to classmates; atypical humor	Asynchrony; unusual interests and passions	Possibly ASD, social (pragmatic) communication disorder
Distractibility; failure to complete tasks; refusal to do schoolwork	Daydreaming; active imagination; needing to be challenged intellectually	Possibly ADHD; learning disability; CAPD
Stubbornness; difficulty with transitions	Independence; high expectations; deep interests; driven to learn	Possibly OCPD; ASD
Emotional intensity; moodiness; argumentativeness	High sensitivity; intensity; asynchrony; need for increased challenge	Possibly mood disorder; ODD
Atypical sleep pattern	Needing little sleep; insufficient stimulation at school; learning more interesting than sleeping	Possibly sleep disorder; ADHD; mood disorder
Atypical eating pattern	Learning more interesting than eating; aversion to some food textures; strong food preferences	Possibly food allergies; sensory processing disorder; eating disorder; mood disorder

Note: This chart should not be read as either-or. As explored in chapter 6, many gifted children are twice-exceptional: gifted with learning disabilities or other diagnoses. Early diagnosis and treatment can be life-changing. If these traits appear at home as well as at school, or if they are more apparent than in other gifted children, further evaluation is warranted.

While the questions and table can be useful, whether a child should have a diagnosis is not always clear because bright children and adolescents are complex. For example, Andrew (mentioned earlier in this chapter) has many characteristics typical of bright children and also many that argue for diagnosis. Such complex situations often

> Understanding the development of bright individuals and assessing their responses in various contexts can reduce the possibility of misdiagnosis.

require more than an interview and a thorough developmental history. Neuropsychological evaluation by a professional trained to recognize characteristics associated with high ability can provide a comprehensive understanding of Andrew, including his cognitive abilities, academic achievement levels, attention and executive functioning skills (ability to plan, organize, and initiate behavior), visual-motor dexterity, and social processing skills. Neuropsychological evaluation also includes gathering information through behavioral questionnaires for Andrew, his parents, and his teacher(s). In addition, testing can reveal how advanced Andrew's thinking and academic skills are (pertinent not only to educational placement, but also to social challenges); whether he has attention and executive functioning difficulties regardless of setting and placement; if his poor handwriting is the result of visual-motor challenges (dysgraphia) or from rushing; and whether he has age-expected social processing skills or challenges related to ASD or social (pragmatic) communication disorder (delays in using social communication).

IMPACT OF MISDIAGNOSIS

When a psychiatric diagnosis is incorrectly assigned, pathology becomes the focus and strengths are often ignored. In such cases, the focus is on what is "wrong" with the child instead of what is "right." In addition, when giftedness is ignored, the bright child is unable to integrate giftedness into identity, often internalizing negative attributes and a feeling of being "too sensitive" and "too intense," for example (Webb et al. 2016). On the other hand, inappropriately attributing all problematic characteristics and behaviors to intelligence is a disservice when an underlying mental health or developmental issue is contributing to impairment. Blaming high ability for problems can affect a child's self-esteem, sense of self, and ability to perform optimally. Ultimately, understanding the development of bright individuals and assessing their responses in various contexts can reduce the possibility of misdiagnosis and instead promote appropriate differentiation, accommodation, and intervention. Accurate assessment, including of complexities associated with high ability, may also help to avoid missing concerns that warrant a diagnosis and treatment.

POINTS TO PONDER

- Characteristics of bright individuals can be misunderstood as pathology.

- Clinical symptoms can be misattributed to giftedness, with legitimate diagnoses missed.

- Understanding the social and emotional characteristics of bright kids is key to determining whether a behavior is related to their unique profile or argues for diagnosis.

- Changing the environment and peer group may improve problematic behavior.

- Accurately diagnosing, and avoiding misdiagnosing, bright children and teens can positively affect their identity and development.

Parenting

ELLE has one of the highest IQ scores in her high school class of more than five hundred students, yet her several D final grades make her an extreme underachiever—seemingly by choice. Her calm appearance, alert expression, and compliance belie her social feistiness and internal turmoil, and her good-humored interaction with classmates and friends in a weekly discussion group for bright kids doesn't suggest anything other than "a good kid," "normal." Her rebellion is relatively undramatic, not reckless. Socializing with friends and spending time with her boyfriend are her priorities. Her high SAT scores make college possible.

Two years later, she and her boyfriend dissolve their three-year relationship, and in a letter to her parents about him she writes, "Our relationship did wonders for my self-esteem, but we grew up to be different people." A stable new relationship lasts beyond college. A year after high school graduation, she has accomplished three main developmental tasks (autonomy, mature relationship, resolution of conflict with parents). A year later, she has direction, a fourth task, behind her. She does well academically throughout college. One day, during her final semester at a state university, she makes a surprise end-of-day visit to a former teacher who supported her when she was keeping her family at bay. She says she is especially grateful to her parents, who "put up with a lot, but let me find myself in ways I needed to. They're very proud of me in what I've accomplished."

Is parenting a bright child different from parenting a typical child in the general population? In some ways, the answer is no. All children need love, support, protection, food, shelter, guidance, structure, and boundaries. However, based on our decades of working with bright kids professionally and raising our own, we believe that parenting a bright child does indeed present some distinct challenges.

All bright kids differ from most of their age peers, of course, given their position on the bell curve of intellectual ability. They tell us they *feel* different. People who observe or interact with them probably see them as different. But personalities and individual characteristics also differ among bright kids. In this chapter we highlight some characteristics that might not be obvious to others and share ideas about how parents and guardians can foster bright kids' positive growth with limited conflict.

HIERARCHY

One trait that often appears early in life for bright individuals is not understanding social, family, and peer hierarchies. We often hear their parents say, "My child doesn't seem to understand that we are in charge." We hear similar comments from teachers, coaches, grandparents, and other adults in positions of authority. Many bright kids don't understand why someone is permitted to tell them what to do just because they are older or have a special position. Their questioning of this social reality is a reminder that the world is geared to hierarchy and compliance.

Children are supposed to listen to their parents, teachers, and coaches and do what they are told, right? Bright kids may not think so. We have observed that they need information before they are willing to comply with adult requests. Barking orders usually doesn't work. A command or request needs to make sense, and the person commanding or requesting needs to respect the child or teen. These complexities make parenting bright kids relatively more complicated and make thought before action essential.

Children are supposed to listen to their parents, teachers, and coaches and do what they are told, right? Bright kids may not think so.

If you are a teacher, parent, counselor, or coach or activity director of a bright, intense, sensitive child or teen, we encourage you to take a moment to consider two important questions: When do you usually get the best compliance, and when the most resistance? Many bright kids believe their rights and adults' rights are similar and that it is unfair for them to have fewer just because they are younger. It's a justice issue for them. They want to know why they are being asked to do something (just as adults do) and are more likely to agree to do it if they are not feeling bossed or controlled (just as adults are). So an interaction is likely to be successful when bright kids are treated with respect and information. The information appeals to their cognitive strengths.

Parents and other invested adults probably have witnessed intense concern about fairness in bright children and teens. Authoritarian parenting and leadership approaches are often not effective with these kids, and power struggles may quickly devolve into yelling, everyone involved feeling bad, and desired outcomes not accomplished. Bright children want to know why, want to negotiate, and want to have at least some control. Their parents probably eventually modify their parenting approaches—because they must. Meanwhile, friends, relatives, and perhaps even siblings may say that the children are running the household, and the parents are negotiating too much. When Dan describes the intensity and spirit of bright children and teens to parents who are regularly having unwanted battles, he refers to a scene in the 1997 movie *Good Will Hunting*, the story of Will, a young-adult genius working as a custodian at MIT (Massachusetts Institute of Technology). Toward the end of the movie, his psychologist shows Will

Parents who teach their bright children "how the world works" are able to help their children accept what is instead of insisting that the world must be as it should be.

photos he has found in Will's legal records of his bruised and battered body and asks him about them. Will says his foster dad beat him regularly and always asked him if he wanted the stick, the belt, or the wrench. Will always chose the wrench. Why would he do that? Will took what little control of the situation he could. He was saying "Bring it on!" to show he would not back down, even when he was being injured and overpowered. Most of Dan's parent clients resonate with this example. They find that their bright children strongly resist traditional parenting methods; but they resist less and even become cooperative when given explanations and some choice.

HOW THE WORLD WORKS

Bright kids might seem to question everything. They can become fixated on what is "not fair"—for example, why they have to do homework, why kids who know less than they do get better grades, or why adults are upset with them after being corrected by them. They also tend to have strong opinions about what is right and how things should be. Unfortunately, life is often unfair, is not as it should be, and doesn't make sense to a bright child.

Dan has found that parents who teach their bright children "how the world works" are able to help their children accept what *is* instead of insisting that the world must be as it *should* be. Here are some examples of how the world works:

- Teachers are likely to be angry at a student for publicly correcting them, even if the teacher is wrong.

- When bright kids report popular kids for cheating, the latter are likely to be intensely angry and to recruit others to make life miserable for the tattlers.

- Students do not generally get high grades if they know the material but do not submit assigned homework or classwork.

- When kids tease, call other kids names, or physically hurt them, peers may not want to play with them. Even though kids who bully may have power, and may even be seen as popular, they are not necessarily well liked.

- Kids and adults who are nice to teachers and bosses often get more privileges than those who show no interest in people who have authority.

These explanations can help bright children use their intellect and problem-solving ability to make sense of injustices. Statements like these also foster conversations about the world in a way that is not uncomfortably intense and personal. Adults can use them as topics for discussion, rather than as topics for lectures about why a behavior is inappropriate.

PRACTICAL APPROACHES FOR PARENTING BRIGHT KIDS

A Collaborative Approach

Because bright children and teens typically like to feel respected, to feel they have some control, and to believe that life should be fair, it makes sense that they want to have an opinion about and impact on what happens, rather than simply being told what to do. Child psychologist Ross Green's (2014) collaborative problem-solving approach is a useful model for working with bright children and teens, their families, and kids in general. The emphasis is on listening and collaborating. Dan knows of kids who are unwilling to put screens away, take out the trash, do homework, or go to bed on time, but then improve their behavior after being invited to help with a plan. In fact, when given an opportunity to collaborate about rules, they might even be more restrictive than their parents would be. This phenomenon parallels how adults feel at work or elsewhere when invited to be part of the solution to a problem.

The Nurturing Parent Approach

The nurturing parent approach, developed by two Boston College researchers in the early 1990s but still not well known, is especially effective with bright kids. John Dacey and Alex Packer described this approach in their 1992 book *The Nurturing Parent: How to Raise Creative, Loving, and Responsible Children*. In this approach, nurturing refers to nurturing *development*, without overparenting or "helicoptering."

Dacey and Packer set out to discover what contributes to creativity in creative kids. They asked teachers and schools to nominate students who had produced highly creative products. They conducted extensive interviews with one thousand of these students and fifty-six parents. Unexpectedly, the parents (who did not know each other) had similar parenting characteristics. In addition, these highly creative kids were described as being responsible, kind, and likeable. No particular kinds of intelligence were explicitly discussed.

The parenting style that emerged from the language of parents and their creative children and teens can be described as respecting children's thoughts and feelings and encouraging them to choose their own priorities rather than having priorities chosen for them. The parents in the study appeared to value and encourage self-discipline, commitment, and intellectual and creative freedom. They let their kids learn from experience rather than through consequences assigned after errors or missteps in behavior or judgment. They believed children needed responsibility to become responsible and needed to make their own decisions to learn good judgment.

Parents of creative children in the study had the following six characteristics:

- They *trusted* their children's sense of fairness and good judgment.
- They *respected* their children's autonomy, thoughts, and feelings.
- They *supported* their children's interests and goals.
- They *enjoyed* their children's company.
- They *protected* their children from hurting themselves or others.
- They *modeled* self-control, sensitivity, and values they believed were important.

These characteristics line up well with key ideas in our book. Bright kids often want equal footing with adults and may be hypersensitive about feeling disrespected. Bright kids usually respond well to those who show them respect. The parents in the Dacey and Packer study supported their bright children's passionate interests and personal strengths. Instead of just tolerating and controlling their children, these parents enjoyed their children, who in turn felt valued. These parents did not abdicate their responsibility to protect their kids by setting needed limits and boundaries. They modeled what they wanted their children to emulate. The researchers found that these families actually had fewer rules than did other families they had studied. During our decades with bright children and their families, we have concluded that the nurturing parent approach is effective for raising healthy and fulfilled bright children, who can become healthy and fulfilled bright adults.

> Bright kids are focused on fairness and want to be treated on equal footing with adults. Bright kids usually respond well to those who show them respect.

HOW TO HELP BRIGHT KIDS BECOME ANXIOUS AND UNBALANCED

In contrast to the behaviors in the nurturing parent approach, some parent behaviors can push bright children in the opposite direction. In workshops and presentations to parents and educators, Jean sometimes includes a slide titled "How to Help Gifted Kids Become Anxious and Unbalanced." The information on it is not intended to blame parents when their bright kids have tense, worried, perfectionistic tendencies. Instead, it is meant to provoke thought about how parents might inadvertently encourage these tendencies in their children and teens:

- focusing only on performance, not on well-being, including at the end of the school day
- talking about goals, products, and performance and not about satisfaction and enjoyment
- insisting on perfection in children who are already showing perfectionistic tendencies

- demeaning play as an unworthy use of time
- overstructuring children's lives and leaving little time for relaxing and thinking outside the box, including about how to spend their time
- sending paradoxical messages like *be the best* or *be number one,* coupled with *you need to relax and be more social, you should have more friends,* or *you should go to bed earlier*
- forgetting children's age—and the social, emotional, and other developmental tasks and challenges that are common at that age

WHAT PARENTS DO MATTERS

We support the idea that to raise bright children who are happy, healthy, and engaged, it is important for parents to reflect on their own continuing development. These kids are sensitive and observant, always watching, absorbing, and thinking about what their parents and other adults say, do, feel, react to, and engage with.

Intentional or unintentional parental modeling can have impact. For example, parents might model frugality, punctuality, trust, self-care, a strong work ethic, healthful eating, involvement in a faith community, and interest in local, national, and international news. When parents do not shame, intimidate, and humiliate their children in order to be in control or to demand "respect," they do not generate fear. If children and teens mirror what parents do not like in themselves, and if parents can avoid reacting to these behaviors and emotions with anger, kids are likely to trust their parents and respond to questions about thoughts and feelings without discomfort. Through such interactions, they can develop expressive language and feel and communicate emotions.

Helping bright kids see other people's perspectives enables them to live in the real world. Modeling nonpatronizing respect for racial, cultural, and economic diversity, even in casual conversation, can affect how a child or teen interacts with people from diverse cultural backgrounds currently and in the future. When parents also help their kids understand that intelligence comes in many forms, and that each form has its own bell curve, kids can learn to respect peers' strengths and talents that are not in the same areas as theirs are. All students in their school need and want respect, friendship, and support. Parents can help their bright, sensitive kids embrace that reality—and that complexity. When parents welcome and affirm their children's peers, when parents encourage their kids to become acquainted with peers who are "different" in any of a multitude of ways, and when parents encourage their bright kids to support ostracized classmates and targets of bullying, they may develop important leadership skills for helping improve the climate of both school and community.

What parents do in their own lives, day after day, can help their children. Although parents of bright children may be anxiously consumed with helping their children deal with school and life, it is also important for parents to focus on their own well-being so they can model self-care for their children. Parents can sometimes feel overwhelmed by their bright children's needs and struggles and be preoccupied with those needs. But those parents who focus enough on their own lives—that is, they "have a life"—can affect their bright children positively, showing them how to live, follow strong interests, feel and express emotions, and persevere in the face of adversity. When parents can express emotions in ways that do not harm other people, self-reflect nonjudgmentally about their and their family's emotional life, and seek counseling for self and family when needed, they may not only be able to calm a tense situation at home but also model effective coping for their bright, anxious, and intense children and teens.

PARALLEL DEVELOPMENT

As a counselor fascinated with development, Jean has sometimes commented, with audiences and clients, that every member of every family is continually developing, part of a complex, evolving dynamic. Not only is each child and teen growing and changing, but young and older adults who live in the home also have developmental concerns related to life satisfaction, sense of fulfillment, building and maintaining a trusting relationship with a significant other, and having a comfortable relationship with parents, in-laws, and adult siblings. These adults might

> Every member of every family is continually developing, part of a complex, evolving dynamic.

not acknowledge what they are wrestling with when moving from one decade of adulthood to the next. However, adult developmental hurdles related to job or career changes, family relocation, decisions about marriage status, care of aging parents and grandparents, health challenges, financial concerns, fears or eagerness related to retirement, accomplishments not yet realized, and avocational paths not taken (to name just a few challenges and concerns) are likely not far from their consciousness.

Jean has seen that bright, sensitive parents may be quite anxious when their kids reach an age that reminds them of their own history. They may recall personal experiences with social awkwardness, struggles with bullying, family relocation, friends who moved away, teachers who did not seem to "get" them, homework stress, embarrassment in physical education classes, or hospitalizations. As noted in chapter 7, it is easy for parents to inadvertently communicate angst from their own past social and academic life to their children as the latter navigate the growing-up years.

In contrast, parents who monitor their own emotions can model effective self-regulation for their intense bright kids. Before focusing on helping their upset child self-regulate, they can regulate themselves. Reflecting on this point in a counseling session focused on memories related to safety and security, Anumeha, a middle-aged woman, recalled her experience at age six, when a home in her neighborhood burned at night. The young owners escaped, but with injuries. The pets did not survive. In retrospect, she

> Wise parents show children that love and acceptance are not dependent on performance, such as grades, awards, or perfect behavior.

gave credit to her mother, who sometimes otherwise struggled dramatically with severe anxiety, for being able to be "an unusually calm mom" after the fire when her kids had trouble sleeping. She gave them age-appropriate information about smoke detectors, fire departments, and kitchen and fireplace safety and assured the kids that their parents would keep them safe. Soon she organized a family fire drill with a game-like format and a little oral quiz afterward.

A common developmental phenomenon in families of bright kids is that these kids can seem so adultlike that awed adults give them too much responsibility in the home. In some homes, by necessity, capable kids are in charge of meals, grocery buying, and clothes washing. They might also become confidants to lonely parents and be asked too seriously for advice. Parents of bright kids need to remember that treating them too deferentially can actually contribute to a sense of insecurity. If financial security falters or health declines in a family member, or if some other tragedy occurs, a bright, sensitive child or teen who is treated like a "little adult" might worry about the family's fate and wonder what they might need to do. When parents shoulder their appropriate parental roles, their kids are likely to be able to act their age and feel secure that the adults in the home will protect and nurture them in crises.

PARENTING SUGGESTIONS

Here are several suggestions to help adults parent their bright kids:

- **Develop listening and responding skills.** Chapter 3 offers suggestions for developing listening and responding skills, which can help parents enter the world of a child or teen respectfully. Good listening invites conversation and helps the listener learn from the speaker, who then becomes the teacher. Good listening models an important relationship skill. It requires hard work and concentration. With good listening skills, parents do not rush in to fix a situation. Wise parents also recognize that a child or teen may need only a good listener, not a problem-solver.

- **Try to communicate unconditional love and acceptance.** Wise parents show children that love and acceptance are not dependent on performance, such as grades, awards, or perfect behavior. They avoid making kids' achievements central to parental self-esteem or compensation for their own school experiences. They do not overvalue what their children accomplish, but they clearly pay attention to it. When a child or teen comes home from school, these parents avoid asking questions like *Did you get an A on the test?* Instead, the first comment might be *Tell me about your day. What did it feel like? What did you notice?*

- **Support the trip, not just the destination.** That is, parents can support the process (*Those small steps you just took with your project—you made them thoughtfully. Let's pause and* *appreciate that.*), not just the final product (*Your teacher should like it. I hope you get an A.*). To avoid fostering preoccupation with external evaluation, parents can encourage nongraded activities in the home and community. They can model focusing on the *process* of whatever they are doing at home or at work—enjoying preparation and construction, not worrying about and talking only about the final critique.

- **Take note of your negative parental messages.** The sensitivities of bright kids can make a negative comment sound like a thunderclap. These kids are probably already highly self-critical. Using demeaning, blaming, or shaming language exacerbates doubts about self-worth. Avoiding critical, negative language might help change cross-generational family habits and decrease stress levels at home.

- **Model effective coping with stress.** Irritability and criticism, anger and a foul temper, chronically condemning a workplace boss during conversation at home, abusing alcohol or other drugs, withdrawing from the family, or passive-aggressive inaction are all inef- fective coping modes that may be harmful to others. Much more helpful is unambiguous expression of feelings. For example, a parent worried about a relative's poor health can simply say so instead of using a hard-edged mood to express anxiety. A parent can validate kids' feelings by simply noticing and naming them with an uncritical tone: *I can hear your frustration. It makes sense that you're angry.* Demonstrating that it's okay to feel, that feelings can be survived, that feelings do change, and that feeling and expressing emotions some- times requires practice is good modeling for kids. Deciding to talk with a counselor for guidance about coping with stress demonstrates that asking for help is not only acceptable, but important.

- **Model play.** Bright kids might hear only that they need to reach their potential—and that they need to focus relentlessly on that vague but serious goal. For balance, wise parents encourage their bright kids and the entire family to take time out to play—at least now and then.

- **Model being kind to yourself after making mistakes.** Wise parents develop a habit of making comments like *I was wrong. Oops!* or *That was sort of clumsy, huh. I do that now and then. Silly me!* Light-hearted self-deprecation can reduce the pressure some kids feel to be good, perfect, and free from error.

- **Give kids permission to explore.** Parents can help their children become independent and confident by taking reasonable risks without fearing failure. For example, parents can encourage them to view classes that might be difficult, an experience in an unfamiliar area of the arts, or social situations that might feel uncomfortable as adventures.

- **Let kids organize their own lives to the extent they are able.** Letting them use their creativity to conquer boredom and make decisions without adult suggestions helps them develop healthy autonomy and gives them a creative outlet. Overinvolving kids in activities and filling their young lives to the brim may be mostly about parental control, not about building character and fostering talent development.

- **Model respect for others.** Disparaging people in authority and societal institutions may encourage cynicism in bright children and teens. Instead, parents can use respectful language to help kids understand social systems, engage them as "anthropologists," and invite them to come home at the end of the school day with insights about how the school functions and how teachers manage so many levels of ability in classes and such varied interests in kids.

- **Teach kids to notice and respect students with interests and skills differing from their own.** Parents can offer to collaborate with someone at school to organize a field trip for a small group of bright kids to a school or business that represents a different kind of intelligence than is usually associated with being bright. For example, a parent might plan a visit to a facility where people repair sophisticated automotive systems.

- **Broaden kids' horizons.** If parents have expertise in a poorly understood professional area, they can offer to make a presentation about it to a classroom of bright kids to help them see applications of what they are learning and to raise awareness of career options.

- **Model not shooting yourself in the foot.** Bright kids need to learn how to get what they need from the system. Speaking and advocating respectfully and wisely with teachers and administrators make it more likely that needs will be met. Parents are wise to remember that good teaching requires great investment of time, energy, and compassionate attention. Accusations and entitled attitudes are not effective when advocating for change or services.

- **Try not to be a needy parent.** Instead of putting a child or teen into a position of taking care of parents' social and emotional needs, parents who are emotionally secure can usually validate anger and other strong feelings in their kids, remain calm when anger is directed at them as parents, and keep the focus on the well-being of the children or teens.

- **Encourage the kids to talk with *someone*.** If kids are hesitant to talk with their parents, their well-being might sometimes depend on having permission to talk with someone else.

- **Beware of overfunctioning.** Overfunctioning means being overly responsible for others. As a parent, it means doing for kids what they are capable of doing for themselves, such as bringing to school an assignment or lunch or gym clothes forgotten at home, putting socks on a six-year-old because the bus is a block away, talking with a teen's teacher about a classroom concern when the teen is capable of self-advocating, or writing an essay for a scholarship application because the teen is procrastinating. Overfunctioning can foster dependence and preclude developing resilience.

- **Remember your kid's age.** Bright kids' adultlike knowledge, insights, and language skills can tempt adults to forget that bright kids are fundamentally still kids. Socially and emotionally, they may be "average" or even "behind." They need parents and guardians to be parents and guardians.

POINTS TO PONDER

- Bright children often feel equal to adults and want to know *why* they need to do what adults tell them to do.

- Collaborating with bright children and treating them with respect are components of effective parenting.

- Teaching bright children how the world works helps them understand and respond to situations they perceive to be unfair and unjust.

- Being self-aware and modeling positive behavior and effective coping are key components of parenting effectively.

Reflecting

An apt mantra to guide interactions with bright kids, and to remember the main points of this book, is simple: *embrace complexity*. In our various roles, we authors have not only observed and been challenged by the complexity of high ability; we have also witnessed the powerful effects of being open to learning about it.

We hope we have helped our readers make sense of bright kids. In turn, we hope they will be able to help these kids make sense of themselves. We have learned about the complex internal world of bright kids *from* bright kids themselves. They are highly idiosyncratic, not easy to categorize, often surprising, rich with insights, and usually unaware of how much they have in common with their intellectual peers—because they have not connected with them genuinely. Each has a public image to protect, after all, and therefore they are likely to hide stress and distress at home or at school, or in both contexts.

Bright kids' complexity reflects more than just their brains and the behaviors and emotions that seem to characterize high ability. Their family circumstances, life events, stressors, and adult and peer models all have impact on their social and emotional development, including their development of identity, autonomy, relationships, direction, and sense of competence.

We come from fields that differ in many ways, yet we view bright kids similarly. We focus on the whole child, rather than solely on academic performance or nonperformance. School achievement, in academic and talent areas, is only a part of the whole, certainly not the essence or ultimate worth of a bright child or teen. In our clinical work, parents and guardians usually don't seek us out for strictly academic reasons. Well-being involves more than academic success.

We both have often used a psychoeducational approach to address concerns in gifted-education classrooms, in summer programs for bright kids, and in our clinical work with them. We give them information based on our clinical experiences and our own and others' research. In group discussions, we might provide psychoeducational information to punctuate what group members have already demonstrated and discussed—or leave it to them to summarize what should be underscored.

Our book reflects our respect for bright kids' desire to understand themselves. These kids invariably welcome information about how a hyperalert, hypersensitive brain works; where they land on a bell curve of general or domain-specific cognitive ability; when sadness warrants a diagnosis and help; how the brain can go into overdrive with anxiety; which categories of misdiagnoses are common to high ability; unique strengths associated with shyness; and what twice-exceptionality means, for example. A comment about the asset-burden paradox of giftedness always makes sense to them. A comment that they aren't "crazy" does as well—followed by explanation of heightened sensitivities and intensities. Informational comments about hiding distress, fearing mistakes and failure, being hesitant to take risks, social challenges, personal boundaries—all of these invariably resonate.

Our book is about development, which we keep in mind as we interact with bright kids. Development is constant, and developmental progress is gradual. We recognize that these kids, on average, vary considerably from grade to grade, including in what energizes them in activities and discussions about social and emotional development. Routinely, they are relieved to know that all bright kids are challenged by growing up. That realization is often a major first step toward well-being, or toward *maintaining* well-being and *preventing* serious concerns. Neither high-achieving nor underachieving bright kids will stay exactly the same as they move into adulthood. Surprises are likely, and there will be bumps in the road, but they and their parents can stay optimistic about the future.

As clinical professionals, we're in sync, even though our approaches differ in some ways. Jean's counseling roots are reflected in her generally nondirective approach—asking open-ended questions, avoiding specific instructions, artfully empowering bright kids to resolve their own problems, and being nonjudgmental and strengths-focused. As an educator of counselors, she helped them curb impulses to talk about themselves—so that the focus stays on the person seeking help. As a clinician, she focuses on developmental tasks, when appropriate, and celebrates developmental progress. She also calls attention to the counseling *process* and to *progress* in counseling, more than to outcomes, along the way.

Dan, as a clinical psychologist, is more likely to develop goals collaboratively with young clients. He is also likely to be less personally neutral, discreetly sharing personal information when it is relevant and when it is likely to relieve a child's or teen's anxiety and normalize developmental challenges. Our similarities and differences led to stimulating discussions as we created this book. His expertise related to assessment, twice-exceptionality, diagnosis, and misdiagnosis allowed us to include those important dimensions credibly in our book.

We wanted our book to offer more than generalities, platitudes, and vague "truths" about high ability. We hope it will help adults interact with bright, complicated kids comfortably; explore their internal world respectfully, collaboratively, and without voyeurism; and be informed advocates for services and support. Ideally, caring adults stand beside kids during tough and confusing times, so that the kids can emerge with increased resilience, a stronger sense of who they are, and optimal emotional health. Adults who care about bright, complicated kids can apply what we offer here, learn more from the kids themselves, and embrace their awesome complexity.

References

Adderholt, Miriam, Donna Johnson, and Nathan Levy. 2015. *Perfectionism vs. the Pursuit of Excellence: What Can Be Bad About Being Too Good.* Monroe Township, NJ: Nathan Levy Books.

Amend, Edward R., and Daniel B. Peters. 2012. "Misdiagnosis and Missed Diagnosis of Gifted Children: The Importance of Accurate Assessment." In *Handbook for Counselors Serving Students with Gifts and Talents: Development, Relationships, School Issues, and Counseling Needs/Interventions,* edited by Tracy L. Cross and Jennifer Riedl Cross, 585–596. Waco, TX: Prufrock Press.

American Psychiatric Association. 2013. *Diagnostic and Statistical Manual of Mental Disorders.* 5th ed. Arlington, VA: Author.

Baldwin, Lois, Susan Baum, Daphne Pereles, and Claire Hughes. 2015. "Twice-Exceptional Learners: The Journey Toward a Shared Vision." *Gifted Child Today* 38 (4): 206–214.

Centers for Disease Control and Prevention (CDC). 2019. "Data and Statistics About ADHD." cdc.gov/ncbddd/adhd/data.html.

Cross, Tracy L., and Cross, Jennifer Riedl. 2012. *Handbook for Counselors Serving Students with Gifts and Talents.* Waco, TX: Prufrock Press.

Csikszentmihalyi, Mihaly. 1997. *Finding Flow: The Psychology of Engagement with Everyday Life.* New York: Basic Books.

Dacey, John S., and Alex J. Packer. 1992. *The Nurturing Parent: How to Raise Creative, Loving, and Responsible Children.* New York: Fireside.

Daniels, Susan, and Michael M. Piechowski. 2009. *Living with Intensity: Understanding the Sensitivity, Excitability, and Emotional Development of Gifted Children, Adolescents, and Adults.* Scottsdale, AZ: Great Potential Press.

Davidson Institute for Talent Development. 2020. "IQ and Educational Needs." Accessed June 25. presskit.ditd.org/Davidson_Institute_Press_Kit/ditd_IQ_and_Educational_Needs.html.

Desmet, Ophélie Allyssa, Nielsen Pereira, and Jean S. Peterson. 2020. "Telling a Tale: How Underachievement Develops in Gifted Girls." *Gifted Child Quarterly,* 64 (2): 85–99.

Duckworth, Angela. 2016. *Grit: The Power of Passion and Perseverance.* New York: Simon and Schuster.

Dweck, Carol. 2016. *Mindset: The New Psychology of Success.* Updated ed. New York: Random House.

Gagné, Françoys. 2018. "Academic Talent Development: Theory and Best Practices." In *APA Handbook of Giftedness and Talent,* edited by Steven I. Pfeiffer, 163–183. Washington, DC: American Psychological Association.

Gardner, Howard. 2006. *Multiple Intelligences: New Horizons.* New York: Basic Books.

Garfield, Craig F., E. Ray Dorsey, Shu Zhu, Haiden A. Huskamp, Rena Conti, Stacie B. Dusetzina, Ashely Higashi, James M. Perrin, Rachel Kornfield, and G. Caleb Alexander. 2012. "Trends in Attention Deficit Hyperactivity Disorder Ambulatory Diagnosis and Medical Treatment in the United States, 2000–2010." *Academic Pediatrics* 12 (2): 110–116.

Gates, Jillian C. 2009. "Diagnosing AD/HD Instead of Identifying Giftedness." *2e Twice-Exceptional Newsletter* 36: 8–10.

Gilman, Barbara Jackson, Dierdre V. Lovecky, Kathi Kearney, Daniel B. Peters, John D. Wasserman, Linda Kreger Silverman, Michael G. Postma, Nancy M. Robinson, Edward R. Amend, Michelle Ryder-Schoeck, Patricia Hedges Curry, Sally K. Lyon, Karen B. Rogers, Linda E. Collins, Gerry M. Charlebois, Colleen M. Harsin, and Sylvia B. Rimm. 2013. "Critical Issues in the Identification of Gifted Students with Co-Existing Disabilities: The Twice-Exceptional." *SAGE Open.* doi:10.1177/2158244013505855.

Gilman, Barbara Jackson, and Dan Peters. 2018. "Finding and Serving Twice-Exceptional Students: Using Triaged Comprehensive Assessment and Protections of the Law." In *Twice-Exceptional: Supporting and Educating Bright and Creative Students with Learning Difficulties,* edited by Scott Barry Kaufman, 19–47. New York: Oxford University Press.

Ginsburg, Kenneth R. 2015. *Building Resilience in Children and Teens: Giving Kids Roots and Wings.* 3rd ed. Elk Grove Village, IL: American Academy of Pediatrics.

Green, Ross W. 2014. *The Explosive Child: A New Approach for Understanding and Parenting Easily Frustrated, Chronically Inflexible Children.* 5th ed. New York: HarperCollins.

Greenspon, Thomas S. 2016. "Helping Gifted Students Move Beyond Perfectionism. *Teaching for High Potential,* November: 10–12.

Grobman, Jerald. 2006. "Underachievement in Exceptionally Gifted Adolescents and Young Adults: A Psychiatrist's View." *Journal of Secondary Gifted Education* 17 (4): 199–210.

Hébert, Thomas P. 1995. "Coach Brogan: South Central High School's Answer to Academic Achievement." *Journal of Secondary Gifted Education* 7 (1): 310–323.

———. 2000. "Defining Belief in Self: Intelligent Young Men in an Urban High School." *Gifted Child Quarterly* 44 (2): 91–114.

———. 2001. "Jermaine: A Critical Case Study of a Gifted Black Child Living in Rural Poverty." *Gifted Child Quarterly* 45 (2): 85–103.

———. 2018. *Talented Young Men Overcoming Tough Times: An Exploration of Resilience.* Waco, TX: Prufrock Press.

HH Dalai Lama and Howard C. Cutler. 2009. *The Art of Happiness: A Handbook for Living, 10th Anniversary Edition.* New York: Riverhead Books.

Jackson, P. Susan, and Jean S. Peterson. 2003. "Depressive Disorder in Highly Gifted Adolescents." *Journal of Secondary Gifted Education* 14 (3): 175–186.

Karpinski, Ruth I., Audrey M. Kinase Kolb, Nicole A. Tetreault, and Thomas B. Borowski. 2018. "High Intelligence: A Risk Factor for Psychological and Physiological Overexcitabilities." *Intelligence* 66: 8–23.

Krafchek, Jennifer, and Leonie Kronborg. 2018. "Stressful Life Events Experienced by Academically High-Achieving Females Before the Onset of Disordered Eating." *Roeper Review* 40 (4): 245–254.

Krafchek, Jennifer, & Leonie Kronborg. 2019 "Academic Emotions Experienced by Academically High-Achieving Females Who Developed Disordered Eating." *Roeper Review* 41 (4): 258–272.

Lythcott-Haims, Julie. 2015. *How to Raise an Adult: Break Free of the Overparenting Trap and Prepare Your Kid for Success.* New York: Henry Holt.

McCoach, D. Betsy, and Del Siegle. 2003. "The Structure and Function of Academic Self-Concept in Gifted and General Education Samples." *Roeper Review* 25 (2): 61–65.

Mendaglio, Salvatore. 2007. "Affective-Cognitive Therapy for Counseling Gifted Individuals." In *Models of Counseling Gifted Children, Adolescents, and Young Adults,* edited by Salvatore Mendaglio and Jean Sunde Peterson, 35–68. Waco, TX: Prufrock Press.

———. 2008. "Dabrowski's Theory of Positive Disintegration: A Personality Theory for the 21st Century." In *Dabrowski's Theory of Positive Disintegration,* edited by Salvatore Mendaglio, 13–40. Scottsdale, AZ: Great Potential Press.

Musgrove, Melody. 2012. OSEP Policy Letter (Redacted). February 29. Washington, DC: US Department of Education, Office of Special Education and Rehabilitative Services (OSEP). ed.gov/policy/speced /guid/idea/letters/2012-1/redacted022912fape1q2012.pdf.

Musgrove, Melody. 2013. Letter to James Delisle. December 20. Washington, DC: US Department of Education, Office of Special Education and Rehabilitative Services (OSEP). ed.gov/policy/speced/guid /idea/memosdcltrs/13-008520r-sc-delisle-twiceexceptional.doc.

National Association for College Admission Counseling (NACAC) and American School Counselor Association (ASCA). 2020. "State-by-State Student-to-Counselor Ratio Report: 10-Year Trends." schoolcounselor.org/asca/media/asca/Publications/ratioreport.pdf.

National Association for Gifted Children (NAGC). 2013. "Position Statement: Comprehensive Assessment to Ensure Gifted Students with Disabilities Receive Appropriate Services." nagc.org/sites /default/files/Position%20Statement/Ensuring%20Gifted%20Children%20with%20Disabilities%20 Receive%20Appropriate%20Services.pdf.

———. 2018. "Position Statement: Use of the WISC-V for Gifted and Twice Exceptional Identification." nagc.org/sites/default/files/Misc_PDFs/WISC-V%20Position%20Statement%20Aug2018.pdf.

———. 2019. "A Definition of Giftedness That Guides Best Practice." nagc.org/sites/default/files /Position%20Statement/Definition%20of%20Giftedness%20%282019%29.pdf.

National Center for Complementary and Integrative Health (NCCIH). 2017. "Autism." nccih.nih.gov /health/autism.

Neumeister, Kristi Speirs. 2016. "Perfectionism in Gifted Students." In *The Social and Emotional Development of Gifted Children: What Do We Know?*, edited by Maureen Neihart, Steven I. Pfeiffer, and Tracy L., 29–39. Waco, TX: Prufrock Press.

Nice, Joanne Bourque. 2006. *Academically Underachieving and Achieving Adolescent Girls: Quantitative and Qualitative Differences in Self-Efficacy, Planning, and Developmental Asynchrony*. York University, Toronto: Unpublished dissertation.

Perou, Ruth, Rebecca H. Bitsko, Stephen J. Blumberg, Patricia Pastor, Reem M. Ghandour, Joseph C. Gfroerer, Sarra L. Hedden, Alex E. Crosby, Susanna N. Visser, Laura A. Schieve, Sharyn E. Parks, Jeffrey E. Hall, Debra Brody, Catherine M. Simile, William W. Thompson, Jon Baio, Shelli Avenevoli, Michael D. Kogan, and Larke N. Huang. 2013. "Mental Health Surveillance Among Children." cdc.gov/mmwr/preview/mmwrhtml/su6202a1.htm.

Peters, Dan. 2013a. *From Worrier to Warrior: A Guide to Conquering Your Fears*. Tucson, AZ: Great Potential Press.

———. 2013b. *Make Your Worrier a Warrior: A Guide to Conquering Your Child's Fears*. Tucson, AZ: Great Potential Press.

———. 2016. The Gifted Child: Misunderstood, Mislabeled, Misdiagnosed. Presented at the American Academy of Pediatrics National Conference and Exhibition, San Francisco, California.

Peters, Dan, Reid, Lisa, and Davis, Stephanie. 2017. *The Warrior Workbook: A Guide for Conquering Your Worry Monster*. Goshen, KY: Great Potential Press.

Peterson, Jean Sunde. 1997. "Bright, Tough, Resilient—And Not in a Gifted Program." *Journal of Secondary Gifted Education* 8 (3): 121–136.

———. 1998. "Six Exceptional Young Women at Risk." *Reclaiming Children and Youth* 6: 233–238.

———. 1999. "Gifted—Through Whose Cultural Lens? An Application of the Postpositivistic Mode of Inquiry." *Journal for the Education of the Gifted* 22 (4): 354–383.

———. 2000a. "A Follow-Up Study of One Group of Achievers and Underachievers Four Years After High School Graduation." *Roeper Review* 22 (4): 217–224.

———. 2000b. "Valuing the Values: Moving from Tolerance to Affirmation." *Reclaiming Children and Youth* 9 (1): 36–40.

———. 2001a. "Gifted and At Risk: Four Longitudinal Case Studies of Post-High-School Development." *Roeper Review* 24 (1): 31–39.

———. 2001b. "Successful Adults Who Were Once Adolescent Underachievers." *Gifted Child Quarterly* 45 (4): 236–250.

———. 2002. "A Longitudinal Study of Post-High-School Development in Gifted Individuals at Risk for Poor Educational Outcomes." *Journal of Secondary Gifted Education* 14 (1): 6–18.

———. 2012. "The Asset-Burden Paradox of Giftedness: A 15-Year Phenomenological, Longitudinal Case Study." *Roeper Review* 34 (4): 244–260.

———. 2014. "Giftedness, Trauma, and Development: A Qualitative, Longitudinal Case Study." *Journal for the Education of the Gifted* 37 (4): 295–318.

———. 2020. *Get Gifted Students Talking: 76 Ready-to-Use Group Discussions About Identity, Stress, Relationships, and More: Grades 6–12*. Minneapolis, MN: Free Spirit Publishing.

Peterson, Jean Sunde, and Nicholas Colangelo. 1996. "Gifted Achievers and Underachievers: A Comparison of Patterns Found in School Files." *Journal of Counseling and Development* 74 (4): 399–407.

Peterson, Jean Sunde, Nancy Duncan, and Kate Canady. 2009. "A Longitudinal Study of Negative Life Events, Stress, and School Experiences of Gifted Youth." *Gifted Child Quarterly* 53 (1): 34–49.

Peterson, Jean Sunde, and Enyi Jen. 2018. "The Peterson Proactive Developmental Attention (PPDA) Model: Nurturing the Rest of the Whole Gifted Child." *Journal for the Education of the Gifted* 41 (2): 111–135.

Peterson, Jean Sunde, and Carrie Wachter Morris. 2010. "Preparing School Counselors to Address Concerns Related to Giftedness: A Study of Accredited Counselor Preparation Programs." *Journal for Education of the Gifted* 33 (3): 163–188.

Peterson, Jean Sunde, and Karen E. Ray. 2006. "Bullying and the Gifted: Victims, Perpetrators, Prevalence, and Effects." *Gifted Child Quarterly* 50 (2): 148–168.

Peterson, Jean S. and Heather Rischar. 2000. "Gifted and Gay: A Study of the Adolescent Experience." *Gifted Child Quarterly* 44 (4): 231–246.

Piechowski, Michael M. 2013. "A Bird Who Can Soar: Overexcitabilities in the Gifted." In *Off the Charts: Asynchrony and the Gifted Child*, edited by Christine S. Neville, Michael M. Piechowski, and Stephanie S. Tolan, 99–122. Unionville, NY: Royal Fireworks Publishing.

Raiford, Susan Engi, Troy Courville, Daniel Peters, Barbara J. Gilman, and Linda Silverman. 2019. *WISC-V Technical Report #6: Extended Norms*. Bloomington, MN: NCS Pearson.

Rapkin, Brett, dir. *The Weight of Gold*. Aired August 19, 2020, on HBO. hbo.com/documentaries /the-weight-of-gold.

Reivich, Karen, and Andrew Shatté. 2002. *The Resilience Factor: 7 Keys to Finding Your Inner Strength and Overcoming Life's Hurdles*. New York: Broadway Books.

Rimm, Sylvia. 2011. "Attention Deficit/Hyperactivity Disorder: A Difficult Diagnosis." In *Parenting Gifted Children*, edited by Jennifer L. Jolly, Donald J. Treffinger, Tracy Ford Inman, and Joan Franklin Smutny, 399–404. Waco, TX: Prufrock Press.

Schuler, Patricia. 2002. "Perfectionism in Gifted Children and Adolescents." In *The Social and Emotional Development of Gifted Children: What Do We Know?*, edited by Maureen Neihart, Sally M. Reis, Nancy M. Robinson, and Sidney M. Moon, 71–79. Waco, TX: Prufrock Press.

Silverman, Linda K. 2013. "Asynchronous Development: Theoretical Bases and Current Applications." In *Off the Charts: Asynchrony and the Gifted Child*, edited by Christine S. Neville, Michael M. Piechowski, and Stephanie S. Tolan, 18–47. Unionville, NY: Royal Fireworks Publishing.

Silverman, Linda K., Barbara J. Gilman, Deirdre V. Lovecky, and Elizabeth Maxwell. 2019. *Teacher Checklist for Recognizing Twice Exceptional Children.* Denver: Gifted Development Center. gifteddevelopment.com/sites/default/files/2019%20Checklist%20for%20Recognizing%202e%20 Children_0.pdf.

US Department of Education Office for Civil Rights. 2016. "Parent and Educator Resource Guide to Section 504 in Public Elementary and Secondary Schools" ed.gov/about/offices/list/ocr/docs/504 -resource-guide-201612.pdf.

Vaivre-Douret, Laurence. 2011. "Developmental and Cognitive Characteristics of 'High-Level Potentialities' (Highly Gifted) Children." *International Journal of Pediatrics* Article ID 420297. doi:10.1155/2011/420297.

Van Gemert, Lisa. 2017. *Perfectionism: A Practical Guide to Managing "Never Good Enough."* Arlington, TX: Gifted Guru Publishing.

Wasserman, John D. 2007. "Intellectual Assessment of Exceptionally and Profoundly Gifted Children." In *High IQ Kids: Collected Insights, Information, and Personal Stories from the Experts*, edited by Kiesa Kay, Deborah Robson, and Judy Fort Brenneman, 48–65. Minneapolis, MN: Free Spirit Publishing.

Webb. James T. 2013. *Searching for Meaning: Idealism, Bright Minds, Disillusionment, and Hope.* Tucson, AZ: Great Potential Press.

Webb, James T., Edward R. Amend, Paul Beljan, Nadia E. Webb, Marianne Kuzujanakis, F. Richard Olenchak, and Jean Goerss. 2016. *Misdiagnosis and Dual Diagnoses of Gifted Children and Adults: ADHD, Bipolar, OCD, Asperger's, Depression, and Other Disorders,* 2nd ed. Tucson, AZ: Great Potential Press.

Weitzman, Carol, and Lynn Wegner. 2015. "Promoting Optimal Development: Screening for Behavioral and Emotional Problems." *Pediatrics* 135 (2): 384–395.

Wood, Susannah M., and Jean Sunde Peterson. 2018. *Counseling Gifted Students: A Guide for School Counselors.* New York: Springer.

Yermish, Aimee. 2010. "Cheetahs on the Couch: Issues Affecting the Therapeutic Working Alliance with Clients Who Are Cognitively Gifted." PhD diss., Massachusetts School of Professional Psychology. davincilearning.org/sketchbook/yermish_2010_gifted_clients_in_therapy.pdf.

Index

About the Authors

Jean Sunde Peterson, Ph.D., is professor emerita and former director of school counselor preparation at Purdue University. In addition to her considerable clinical work with gifted youth, she has conducted workshops and presented keynote addresses internationally on their social and emotional development, with topics related to academic underachievement, prevention- and development-oriented small-group work, listening skills, bullying, and trauma. Dr. Peterson has authored more than 140 books, journal articles, and invited book chapters, and her articles have appeared in all major gifted-education journals as well as in the *Journal of Counseling & Development, Professional School Counseling,* and *International Journal of Educational Reform*. She has received ten national awards for scholarship, including the 2020 Distinguished Scholar Award from the National Association for Gifted Children, as well as twelve awards at Purdue for teaching, research, or service. She was a state teacher of the year in her first career as a classroom teacher. She lives in Indiana.

Daniel B. Peters, Ph.D., is cofounder and executive director of the Summit Center. He has devoted his career to the assessment and treatment of children, adolescents, and families, specializing in overcoming worry and fear, learning differences such as dyslexia, and issues related to giftedness and twice-exceptionality. Dr. Peters is the author of *Make Your Worrier a Warrior*, its companion children's and teen's guide, *From Worrier to Warrior*, and the *Warrior Workbook*. He contributed to *Twice Exceptional: Supporting and Educating Bright and Creative Students with Learning Difficulties* and *toughLOVE: Raising Confident, Kind, Resilient Kids*, coauthored *Raising Creative Kids,* and has authored many articles on topics related to parenting, family, giftedness, twice-exceptionality, dyslexia, and anxiety. He cofounded and codirects Camp Summit, a camp for gifted children, and hosts the *Parent Footprint Podcast with Dr. Dan*. Dr. Peters was recognized as the 2018 Mental Health Professional of the Year by Supporting Emotional Needs of the Gifted (SENG) and received the 2013 Distinguished Service Award from the California Association for Gifted. He lives in Northern California.

Other Great Resources from Free Spirit

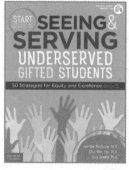

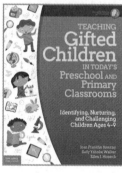